4
College Vocabulary

HOUGHTON MIFFLIN
ENGLISH FOR ACADEMIC SUCCESS

John D. Bunting
Georgia State University

SERIES EDITORS

Patricia Byrd

Joy M. Reid

Cynthia M. Schuemann

Houghton Mifflin Company

Boston   New York

Publisher: Patricia A. Coryell
Director of ESL Publishing: Susan Maguire
Senior Development Editor: Kathy Sands Boehmer
Editorial Assistant: Evangeline Bermas
Senior Project Editor: Kathryn Dinovo
Manufacturing Assistant: Karmen Chong
Senior Marketing Manager: Annamarie Rice
Marketing Assistant: Andrew Whitacre

Cover graphics: LMA Communications, Natick, Massachusetts

Photo credits: © Randy Faris/Corbis, p. 1; © Jose Luis Pelaez, Inc./Corbis, p. 22; © Alan Schein Photography/Corbis, p. 40; © Royalty-Free/Corbis, p. 58; © Reuters/Corbis, p. 79; © Royalty-Free/Corbis, p. 89; © David Turnley/Corbis, p. 99; © Caroline Penn/Corbis, p. 107; © Royalty-Free/Corbis, p. 113.

Text credits:
D. Crystal, The Cambridge Encyclopedia of the English Language. Copyright © 1995. Reprinted with the permission of Cambridge University Press. p. 3; From *The American Heritage English as a Second Language Dictionary*. Copyright © 1998 by Houghton Mifflin Company. Used by permission. p. 10; From Carol Kanar, The Confident Student, pp. 36–37, 225–226, and 226. Copyright © 2004 by Houghton Mifflin Company. Used by permission. pp. 24, 30, 34; www.acceleratedlearningnetwork.com/multiple.htm Adapted from "Accelerated Learning for the 21st Century," by Colin Rose and Malcolm J. Nicholl. New York, NY: Dell, 1998. p. 26; J. Nevid, *Psychology Concepts and Applications*, pp. 629–630, 634–636 and 643–647. Copyright © 2003 by Houghton Mifflin Company. Used by permission. pp. 42, 47, 52; Reprinted with permission of The Markkula Center for Applied Ethics at Santa Clara University. www.scu.edu/ethics. p. 61; Globalization Without a Net, by Vito Tanzi. © 2001 by Foreign Policy. Reproduced with permission of Foreign Policy in the format Textbook via Copyright Clearance Center. For more information visit www.foreignpolicy.com. p. 86; Copyright © 2000 by The New York Times Co. Reprinted with permission. p. 93; From Donella Meadows, "Our 'Footprints' Are Treading Too Much Earth," Charleston SC Gazette, April 1, 1996. Reprinted by permission of Sustainability Institute, on behalf of the Estate of Donella Meadows. p. 103; Stuart L. Hart, "Beyond Greening: Strategies for a Sustainable World," Harvard Business Review, January/February 1997. Reprinted by permission of Harvard Business School Publishing Division. pp. 103, 107; J. Ottman, "Consumers with a Conscience," Green Marketing, 2/e. Reprinted by permission of the author. pp. 113–114.

Printed in the U.S.A.

Library of Congress Control Number: 2004112261

ISBN: 0-618-23027-0

123456789-EUH-08 07 06 05 04

Contents

Houghton Mifflin English for Academic Success Series
- What is the Vocabulary strand all about?   iv
- What student competencies are covered in *College Vocabulary 1–4*?   vi

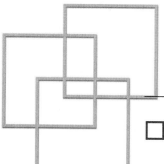

Houghton Mifflin English for Academic Success Series

☐ What Is the Vocabulary Strand All About?

The Houghton Mifflin English for Academic Success series is a comprehensive program of student and instructor materials. There are four levels of student language proficiency textbooks in three skill areas (oral communication, reading, and writing) and a supplemental vocabulary textbook at each level. Knowing how to learn and use academic vocabulary is a fundamental skill for college students. Even students with fluency in conversational English need to become effective at learning academic words for their college courses. All of the textbooks in the Houghton Mifflin English for Academic Success (EAS) series include work on vocabulary as part of academic reading, academic writing, and academic oral communication. In addition, this series provides four Vocabulary textbooks that focus on expanding student academic vocabulary and their skills as vocabulary learners. These textbooks can be used alone or can be combined with a reading, writing, or oral communication textbook. When used with one of the textbooks in the Houghton Mifflin English for Academic Success series, the vocabulary textbooks can be provided at a reduced cost and shrink-wrapped with the reading, writing, or oral communication books.

Academic vocabulary involves two kinds of words: (1) general academic vocabulary that is used in many different disciplines, and (2) highly technical words that are limited to a particular field of study. As they prepare for academic study, students need first to learn generally used academic words. A list of the general academic words called the Academic Word List (AWL) has been published by Averil Coxhead[1]. Coxhead organizes AWL words into lists based on word families, defining a *word family* as a set of related words.

The Vocabulary textbooks prepare students for their academic study by teaching them the meanings and uses of the AWL words. The AWL word families are divided among the four textbooks with each book presenting approximately 143 word families. To see the word lists for each book, visit the website for the vocabulary series at www.college.hmco.com/esl/students.

Learning new words is more effective when words are studied in meaningful contexts. Each chapter in the Vocabulary series contextualizes a set of approximately 25–30 AWL words in a "carrier topic" of interest to students. The carrier topics are intended to make the study more interesting as well as to provide realistic contexts for the words being studied. Learning a new word means learning its meaning, pronunciation, spelling, uses, and related members of the word's family. To help students with these learning challenges, the Vocabulary textbooks provide multiple encounters with words in a wide variety of activity types.

1. The AWL was introduced to the TESL/TEFL world with Coxhead's *TESOL Quarterly* publication: Coxhead, A. (2000). A new academic word list. *TESOL Quarterly 34*(2); 213–238. Coxhead is also the author of the *Essentials of Teaching Academic Vocabulary*, a teacher-reference book in the Houghton Mifflin English for Academic Success series.

Each chapter has been structured to incorporate learning strategies or tips that will help students become active acquirers and collectors of words. Additionally, because research supports the idea that multiple exposures are of great significance in learning vocabulary, each word family is practiced repeatedly and many are recycled in the lessons and chapters that follow their introduction. Newly introduced vocabulary appears in **bold** type. Recycled vocabulary is indicated by a dotted underline.

Student websites for the Vocabulary textbooks provide additional practice with the AWL words as well as useful review chapters. Instructors and students can download these review chapters for use as homework or in-class study. The website for each book expands the practice with the AWL words covered in that book. Students can access vocabulary flash cards for the complete 570 word families if they choose to work with words beyond those introduced in the particular vocabulary textbook they are studying. Each of these flash cards has the AWL word, its definition, and an example.

Although, with the addition of on-line answer keys, this book can be an aid to self-study, it is ideally suited for classroom use. According to the focus of your course, you may choose to have your students respond to some of the exercises in writing, while you may choose to make oral activities of others. Of course, you can also incorporate practice in both skills by following oral discussion with a writing assignment. You may ask students to work individually on some exercises, while others will be better suited to pair or small- group configurations.

Acknowledgments

First, I acknowledge my wonderful students, who have graciously given me the learner's perspective on these activities for learning vocabulary in a second language. I would also like to thank the people at Houghton Mifflin, especially Susan Maguire, Kathy Sands Boehmer, and Evangeline Bermas, for their ability to work with me so patiently throughout this process and to somehow keep me on track. Thanks to Joy Reid, Cynthia Schuemann, and especially Pat Byrd for their enormous efforts in coordinating this project. Thanks also to my reviewers—William Brazda, Long Beach City College; Terese Francis, Doane College; and Shelly Hedstrom, Palm Beach Community College—who took the time to evaluate the manuscript and suggest useful changes. This book would be much weaker if not for the wonderful efforts of my colleagues/advisors Harriet Allison, Lousie Gobron, and especially Frank Smith, who provided me with much needed perspective within a kind and encouraging framework. My two wonderful sons, Chris and James, pulled me away enough times to remind me that work needs to coexist with play, and play we must! Finally, I send my heartfelt appreciation to Mayira Quintero Bunting, to whom this book is dedicated. With your support and love, all is made easy.

☐ What Student Competencies Are Covered in *College Vocabulary 1–4?*

Description of Overall Purposes

Students develop the ability to understand and use words from the Academic Word List (AWL) that are frequently encountered in college course work.

Materials in this textbook are designed with the following minimum exit objectives in mind:

Competency 1: The student will recognize the meaning of selected academic vocabulary words.

Competency 2: The student will demonstrate controlled knowledge of the meaning of selected academic vocabulary words.

Competency 3: The student will demonstrate active use of selected academic vocabulary words.

Competency 4: The student will develop and apply strategies for vocabulary learning. The student will:
   a. recognize roots, affixes, and inflected forms.
   b. distinguish among members of word families.
   c. identify and interpret word functions.
   d. recognize and manipulate appropriate collocations.
   e. use contextual clues to aid understanding.
   f. develop word learning resources such as flash cards and personal lists.
   g. increase awareness of how words are recycled in written text and oral communication.
   h. increase awareness of the benefits of rehearsal for word learning (repetition and reuse of words in multiple contexts).

Competency 5: The student will use dictionaries for vocabulary development and to distinguish among multiple meanings of a word.

Competency 6: The student will analyze words for syllable and stress patterns and use such analysis to aid in correct pronunciation.

Competency 7: The student will analyze words for spelling patterns.

Competency 8: The student will become familiar with web-based resources for learning AWL words.

Vocabulary and Language

In this chapter, you will

- Become familiar with twenty-four high-frequency academic English words
- Identify the different parts of a dictionary entry
- Learn about words in authentic texts and how you can use them to build vocabulary strength
- Look at pronunciation patterns of academic words
- Learn about vocabulary and language

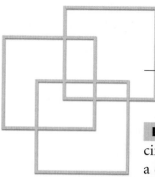

Section 1

EXERCISE 1 For each bold vocabulary word in Word List 1.1, circle the letter with the best definition. Look at the examples, and use a dictionary if necessary.

WORD LIST 1.1

Word/Examples	Definitions
accumulation (*n.*) …a huge *accumulation* of capital in the country …	a. Gathering together b. Loss c. Disappearance
compile (*v.*) …*compile* records/data … …information has been *compiled* …	a. Forget b. Learn c. Put into a list
enormous (*adj.*) …an *enormous* responsibility … …an *enormous* mansion …	a. Angry b. Large c. Wealthy
fluctuations (*n.*) …short-term *fluctuations* in oil prices …	a. Increases b. Consistency c. Changes
guidelines (*n.*) The government provides only general *guidelines* on working conditions.	a. Laws b. Instructions or advice c. Ropes
offset (*n./v.*) Overseas losses were partially *offset* by the strong local market.	a. To destroy something completely b. To balance the affects of something c. To remain neutral in difficult times
preliminary (*adj.*) …*preliminary* results suggest that …	a. At the very end b. Near the middle c. Before something more important
temporary (*adj.*) …the situation is only *temporary* …	a. For a limited time b. Paid for by governments c. Very uncertain

EXERCISE 2   Before reading the following passage, answer these questions.

1. How many words do you need to know in order to speak a language?

_____

_____

2. How many words should you know in order to study at college or university?

_____

_____

3. What does it mean to "know" a word?

_____

_____

_____

_____

Reading 1

HOW MANY WORDS DO YOU KNOW?

Vocabulary researchers have tried to determine the size of the mental lexicon (how many words a person knows) and how a person **accumulates** this **enormous** number of words. It is difficult to **compile** such a number for several reasons. First, the concept of a "word" must be agreed upon, and second, the concept of what it means to "know" a word needs to be satisfactorily defined. General figures for an average native speaker vary widely, and some researchers suggest a **preliminary** figure from 10,000 words up to 25,000 words. This number can be manipulated based on several factors, so we need to set some guidelines for what these numbers mean.

For example, consider the word ***fluctuate***. If you know the verb *fluctuate* and the noun *fluctuation,* would this be counted as one word or two? Add to that the adjective *fluctuating,* and then you have an even larger variation between possible vocabulary sizes. Usually, words that have the same general meaning but can be formed into a number of parts of speech (e.g., noun, verb, adjective, adverb) are counted as one word, or what is sometimes called one **word family**.

Another problem is this: suppose you know the word *bank* as used in the sentence "I went to the bank yesterday to withdraw some money." Yet you also know the meaning in "We enjoy sitting along the bank of the river on Sunday afternoons." If you know two different meanings of the same word (*bank*, in this case), is that two words or one?

A third concern is what it means to 'know' a word. Understanding a word in context in reading is quite different from being able to produce it when you are writing an essay. It is useful to distinguish between *receptive* and *productive* word knowledge, with receptive knowledge usually attached to listening and reading skills, and productive knowledge generally linked to speaking and writing.

What is the size of *your* vocabulary? How would you try to find out? It's not feasible to count every word, so what might you do? One approach has been to randomly select pages from different parts of a dictionary and make a note of whether you know each word on those pages. Therefore, following these **guidelines**, if you were to do this for 10 pages from a 1000-page dictionary (or 1 percent of the dictionary), you would simply multiply the total number of words you know by 100 to get a preliminary idea of your vocabulary size.

Source: Crystal, D. (1995). *The Cambridge Encyclopedia of the English Language.* Cambridge, UK: Cambridge University Press.

EXERCISE 3 Answer the following questions based on Reading 1. In your answers, try to use the vocabulary words given in the parentheses.

1. Have you ever tried to estimate your vocabulary size? With a classmate, try to estimate the size of your vocabulary by using the approach suggested in the reading. Discuss the results. (*compile, preliminary*)

_____

_____

_____

2. With several classmates, create a set of guidelines for building a stronger vocabulary. Compare your guidelines with other students'. (*guidelines*)

_____

_____

_____

_____

EXERCISE 4 Use this pretest to determine your knowledge of the vocabulary words. First, read the category descriptions listed below. Then, in the chart, write each word from the word bank in the category that best describes your understanding of that word. Do not spend more than thirty seconds on each word. For each word you list in the last column ("Use this word in my own writing"), write a sentence with the word to show you understand the word's meaning.

- **Don't know this word at all** means the word is completely unfamiliar to you. You have never seen it before.
- **Recognize this word but don't know well** means you have a sense of the meaning but may not know how it differs from its synonyms.
- **Know this word well** means you feel comfortable with the word and would not need a dictionary to check the meaning.
- **Use this word in my own writing** means you can use the word appropriately in your own writing and speaking.

Source: Nation, I. S. P. (1990). *Teaching and Learning Vocabulary.* New York: Newbury House.

accumulation compile	enormous fluctuation	guideline offset	preliminary temporary

Don't know this word at all	Recognize this word but don't know well	Know this word well	Use this word in my own writing

Master Student Tip

Consider how well you already know a word before you start actively learning it. Pretests for the vocabulary words in this chapter may be found at http://esl.college.hmco.com/students. You may print them out to complete them for each word list.

EXERCISE 5 Write the given vocabulary word that best completes each sentence. Each word is used only once. The first one has been done for you as an example. Use a dictionary to check your answers.

Nouns	
compilation fluctuations guidelines accumulation offset	**1.** The true measure of vocabulary mastery is the _accumulation_ of many vocabulary dimensions, rather than just knowing one meaning of the word. **2.** In vocabulary learning, making a _____ of words you know can help you strategize about learning more. **3.** _____ in price are common in the stock market. **4.** Students should develop _____ for choosing which words are most important to study in depth.
Adjectives	
preliminary enormous temporary accumulative	**5.** Developing a near native vocabulary would result in _____ advantages for students who want to study at a university. **6.** A _____ step to building a strong vocabulary is to understand the many components involved in knowing a word. **7.** *Interlanguage* is a term used for the _____ language that combines your first language with your emerging second language.

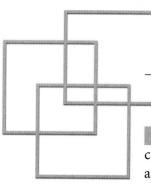

Section 2

EXERCISE **6** For each bold vocabulary word in Word List 1.2, circle the letter of the best definition. Look at the examples, and use a dictionary if necessary.

WORD LIST 1.2

Word/Examples	Definitions
appreciate (*v.*) We truly *appreciate* your efforts.	a. Understand b. Enjoy c. Value
automatically (*adv.*) Most people process their first language *automatically*.	a. Without planning b. Quickly c. For a long period of time
chart (*n.*) …a bar *chart* … …*charts* and graphs …	a. A picture of business products b. A model c. A graphic representation of data
contemporary (*adj.*) …*contemporary* furniture …	a. Old b. Modern c. Expensive
diminish (*v.*) …*diminished* returns on investment …	a. To become smaller b. To be unimportant c. To be unreliable
exploitation (*n.*) …*exploitation* of natural resources …	a. Using something for political gain b. Using something to gain advantage c. Recycling of materials
institute (*v.*) …the firm will *institute* changes …	a. To start b. To recover c. To terminate
manipulation (*n.*) …clever *manipulation* of the facts …	a. Controlling something or someone b. Writing clearly c. Sending people to events

EXERCISE **7** Before reading the following passage, answer these questions.

1. What kind of dictionary do you use now?

_____

_____

2. What kind of information can you find in the dictionary?

_____

_____

_____

Reading 2

USING A DICTIONARY

One of the most important tools for developing a strong academic vocabulary is a dictionary. **Contemporary** learner dictionaries are enormously different from older "traditional" dictionaries. For one thing, almost all new learner dictionaries have **instituted** the use of corpus data (enormous electronic databases of texts from many sources) and defining vocabulary (definitions are written using only a restricted group of common words that learners of English can easily understand). Another useful component of these dictionaries is the wide variety of **charts**, graphs, and illustrations.

Look at this entry from the _American Heritage English as a Second Language Dictionary_ for the word _enormous_. There are many elements of knowing a word, and using a dictionary effectively can help you **manipulate** a word in its meanings, grammar, and associated words. When you understand how useful a dictionary is, you can better **appreciate** what you must know about a word to use it in your writing. If you practice using a dictionary when you are learning new academic words, any worries about your dictionary skills will **diminish**, and you will find that you do it almost **automatically**. A good learner dictionary is a great resource to **exploit** when you want to improve your reading _and_ your writing!

Dictionary entry for enormous

Meanings—
physical and
nonphysical

e·nor·mi·ty (ĭ nôr´mĭ tē) *n.* [U] Very great size or
seriousness: *People were horrified at the enormity
of the crime.*

Count/noncount
nouns

Word forms:

n.–noun

adj.–adjective

adv.–adverb

e·nor·mous (ĭ nôr´məs) *adj.* Very great in size,
extent, number, or degree: *an enormous elephant;
the enormous cost of building a sports arena.* See
Synonyms at **large**. **–e·nor´mous·ly** *adv.*

Grammar structures:
enormity *of the—*

Common word
combinations: *an
enormous [animal],
enormous cost*

Other useful abbreviations in definitions

sthg. = something

sbdy. = somebody

tr.v. = transitive verb (takes an object)

intr.v. = intransitive verb (cannot take an object)

Similar words—
synonyms and
related words

Source: *The American Heritage English as a Second Language Dictionary.* (1998).
Boston: Houghton Mifflin, p. 300.

EXERCISE **8** Use this dictionary entry for *manipulate* to answer
these questions.

Dictionary entry for manipulate

ma·nip·u·late (mə **nĭp**´ye lāt) *tr.v.* **ma·nip·u·lat·ed, ma·nip·u·lat·ing,
ma·nip·u·lates. 1.** To operate or control (sthg.), especially with skill:
The pilot manipulated the controls of the airplane. **2.** To influence or
manage (sbdy./sthg.) in a clever or dishonest way: *He manipulated
public opinion in his favor.* **–ma·nip´u·la´tion** *n.* [C; U]
–ma·nip´u·la´tive (mə **nĭp**´ye lā´tĭv *or* mə **nĭp**´ye lə´tĭv) *adj.*
–ma·nip´u·la´tor *n.*

sbdy. = somebody, *sthg.* = something

Source: *The American Heritage English as a Second Language Dictionary.* (1998).
Boston: Houghton Mifflin, p. 535.

1. What part of speech is *manipulative*?

_____

_____

2. For definition 1, what kinds of things could be manipulated?

_____   _____

_____

_____

_____

3. For definition 2, what kinds of things could be manipulated?

_____

_____

_____

_____

Master Student Tip

Using a good dictionary is important if you want to build a strong, active vocabulary. There are several kinds of dictionaries, which each has its own benefits:

- **A "college" dictionary:** "College" dictionaries are traditional dictionaries. The benefit is that they include many more words than either bilingual or learner dictionaries. However, they do not have much information about grammar or vocabulary patterns. They also usually have definitions that are very difficult to understand.
- **A bilingual dictionary:** A good bilingual dictionary is an excellent tool for accessing information you already have in your first language. However, most bilingual dictionaries do not include information about grammar or vocabulary patterns. They also do not always make clear distinctions between different meanings a word may have.
- **An ESL/EFL learner dictionary:** A learner dictionary provides much useful information about meaning, grammar, and vocabulary patterns. This kind of dictionary usually has different kinds of information about the most common words. They also usually have clear, understandable definitions and useful distinctions between apparent synonyms. One limitation to these dictionaries is that they do not list as many words as college or bilingual dictionaries.

What kind of dictionary do you have? How do you use it? Building good dictionary strategies will help you become an active vocabulary learner.

EXERCISE **9** Answer the following questions based on Reading 2. In your answers, try to use the vocabulary words given in the parentheses.

1. How can you exploit all the information available in a dictionary entry? (*exploit*)

_____

_____

_____

2. If you cannot find information you want in your dictionary, what strategies might you institute? (*institute*)

_____

_____

_____

3. List the ways of knowing a word in diminishing order of importance. Be ready to justify your choices. (*diminish*)

_____

_____

_____

EXERCISE **10** When you are learning a new word, sometimes it can be useful to look at the word in different authentic contexts. You can learn about a word by seeing how it is used in real speech and writing. Read these authentic lines containing the word *appreciative*. Then answer the questions that follow.

- . . . was seen as insufficiently *appreciative* of British efforts . . .
- He was *appreciative* of the kind words but more so . . .
- Mr. Barlow's family were very *appreciative* that his body was found.
- Yes, I was very *appreciative* of that thank you . . .
- Clinton assured an *appreciative* audience at Shevchenko University . . .
- . . . and something we're very *appreciative* of.
- We are very *appreciative* for all the help we have received . . .

■ They agree that the faculty should be *appreciative* of the staff.

■ . . . and I was *appreciative* of them inviting the president . . .

■ RITA: We are most *appreciative* of that opportunity.

■ . . . a fact consumers are not really *appreciative* of and so I think . . .

■ . . . and I'm very, very *appreciative* of the work that my father did . . .

1. What kinds of words (e.g., nouns, verbs) are used before and after *appreciative*?

_____

_____

2. What are the most common adverbs that come right before *appreciative* in the sentences?

_____

_____

3. What preposition usually follows *appreciative*? Create a "rule" for preposition use with the adjective *appreciative*.

_____

_____

_____

_____

Master Student Tip

Noticing a word's frequent patterns is an important way to build your vocabulary. Words have two kinds of patterns: grammatical and lexical. *Grammatical patterns* include prepositions or types of phrases that occur often. *Lexical patterns* are words that combine frequently with a given word (these patterns are also called collocations). It is easier to notice patterns when you see and hear the words again and again. A good strategy for building academic vocabulary is to look for ways to see and hear academic words as often as possible, and to notice other words that are used with them.

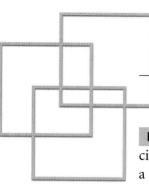

Section 3

EXERCISE 11 For each bold vocabulary word in Word List 1.3, circle the letter of the best definition. Look at the examples, and use a dictionary if necessary.

WORD LIST 1.3

Word/Examples	Meaning
anticipated (*adj.*) . . . widely *anticipated* outcome . . .	a. Undesired b. Hoped for c. Avoided
commodity (*n.*) . . . rising *commodity* prices . . .	a. Stocks b. Economic factors c. Something that can be bought or sold
controversy (*n.*) . . . the current *controversy* surrounding the president . . .	a. A public disagreement b. Fame c. Investigation
distribution (*n.*) . . . the *distribution* of world resources . . .	a. Giving things in equal shares b. Buying and selling c. Moving into unknown areas
indicate (*v.*) . . . recent evidence clearly *indicates* that . . .	a. To show b. To disprove c. To forget
perceive (*v.*) . . . the sound was barely *perceived* . . .	a. To hear b. To understand or realize c. To acknowledge
prospect (*n.*) . . . the *prospect* of finding a job . . .	a. Possibility for something good b. A guarantee c. Finding gold
variables (*n.*) . . . dependent/independent *variables* affect the outcome . . .	a. Factors that never change b. Unknown information c. Changeable elements

EXERCISE 12 Before reading the following passage, answer this question.

What are some ways you can classify or categorize words?

_____

_____

Reading 3

DEFINING A WORD FAMILY

A word family includes all the **various** forms of a word. These usually are the noun (human, abstraction, action, etc.), verb, adjective (active and/or passive), and adverb forms. Not all words have all forms, and some words have more than one choice for each form. Look at the word family for *distribute*:

- Noun—*distribution, distributor*
- Verb—*to distribute*
- Adjective—*distributive*
- Adverb—none

Knowing word families is an important part of vocabulary knowledge. Knowing word forms means you will be able to use a word in any position in a sentence. Look at the word family flash card for *manipulate*.

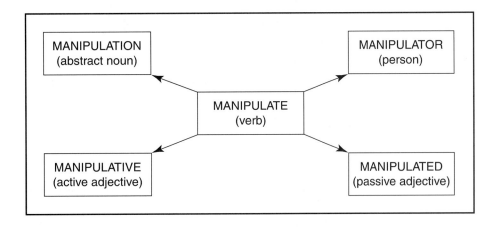

Master Student Tip

Many students benefit from using flash cards. The example here is one way to make flash cards, but it is not the only way. To design your own flash cards, determine what you want to know about a word but find hard to remember. You may make spelling flash cards, pronunciation flash cards, and meaning (and multiple-meaning) flash cards. As you build your vocabulary, experiment with different flash cards. What other kinds of information could you put on a flash card?

EXERCISE 13   Complete the following tasks:

1. Complete the chart by writing word forms for each bold vocabulary word's part of speech. If no word form exists, write "none." After you are done, compare your answers with another student's. Then check in a dictionary for other forms of these words. The first one has been done for you as an example.

Noun	Verb	Adjective	Adverb
anticipation	**anticipated**	anticipated anticipatory	none
commodity			
controversy			
distribution			
	indicate		
	perceive		
prospect			
variables			

2. Choose four words from the *chart* above to create a Word Family flash card (similar to the flash card for *manipulate* above). On one side, write the word; on the other side, write the word family. Use a dictionary to check for any common grammar patterns (like the pattern *appreciative* + *of*), and write them below that word form on the flash card. Use this space to plan out your flash cards.

Master Student Tip

Accurate stress in speaking is important for communicative effectiveness. Pronunciation is an important and often overlooked part of vocabulary learning. English has recurring stress patterns, especially in academic language. One common pattern is found in nouns ending in *-tion*. Many academic words have four syllables, with the main stress on the third syllable:

distribution: dis tri **BU** tion   *indication*: in di **CA** tion
                1 – 2 – **3** – 4   1 – 2 – **3** – 4

One way to identify these patterns is by using two numbers: the number of syllables (one, two, etc.) followed by the number of the stressed syllable (first, second, etc.). For example, the words above, *distribution* and *indication*, would fit the 4–3 pattern (four syllables, with the stress on the third syllable). The words *currency* (CUR ren cy) and *mutual* (MU tu al) would both fit the 3–1 pattern (three syllables, with the stress on the first syllable). Developing an awareness of these patterns will make your pronunciation of academic words more consistent and effective.

EXERCISE **14** Complete the following tasks:

Write stress patterns for the following words. The first one has been done for you as an example. After you are done, use a dictionary to check your work.

1. manipulate   (__4__ – __2__)

2. appreciate   (_____ – _____)

3. contemporary   (_____ – _____)

4. diminished   (_____ – _____)

5. offset   (_____ – _____)

6. preliminary   (_____ – _____)

7. temporarily   (_____ – _____)

8. controversial   (_____ – _____)

9. commodity   (_____ – _____)

10. controversy   (_____ – _____)

11. distribution   (_____ – _____)

12. automatic   (_____ – _____)

Study the stress patterns of the following words. Find and write other words from the chapter that fit the same pattern. You may also add other words you already know. If you are not sure about your answers, use a dictionary.

Word	Pattern	Example 1	Example 2	Example 3
appreciate	4–2			
controversy	4–1			
distribution	4–3	indication		
indicate	3–1			
prospect	2–1			

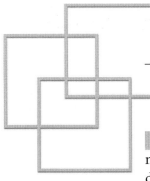

Section 4

CHAPTER 1 REVIEW

EXERCISE 15 Review Chapter 1 Word List. Do you know the meaning of each word? Do you know the part of speech? What different word forms do the words have?

accumulate	compile	exploit	offset
anticipate	contemporary	fluctuate	perceive
appreciate	controversy	guideline	preliminary
automate	diminish	indicate	prospect
chart	distribute	institute	temporary
commodity	enormous	manipulate	vary

EXERCISE 16 Choose the best word given that completes *all* the sentences in each group. You may use a dictionary to check for additional meanings of words.

controversy exploitation perception	**1.** ■ Membership of the EC started the trend, and the breakup of the Warsaw Pact and the Soviet Union has given it a new lease of life as fledgling democracies create markets ripe for _____. ■ Jahangir, her country's foremost human rights advocate, said she expects her struggle for human rights to lead to a "world where people can live a life free of _____." ■ However, the protection of children from sexual _____ by parents was regarded as far more significant. **The best word for this group of sentences is** _____..

accumulation

anticipation

enormity

fluctuations

guidelines

manipulation

2. ■ Wheat futures rose in _____ of subsidized sales of U.S. wheat to Bangladesh and Algeria.

■ By 9:30 a.m. the campsite was buzzing with _____ as everyone made sure that her or his equipment was working.

The best word for this group of sentences is

_____.

3. ■ Concern about the destructiveness of human nature is paralleled by awareness of the _____ of global evil and suffering, aggravated by the potential powers now within human grasp.

■ There are times when the _____ of the challenge makes you want to pull a blanket over your head.

■ Because of the _____ of the problem that hazardous wastes present, a large fund will be needed to cope with cleanup.

The best word for this group of sentences is

_____.

4. ■ "You can see from the report that the margin is decreasing and this is in line with what we say about currency _____ being the main cause of the difference in prices of cars between the UK and the rest of Europe."

■ Local _____ in price are usually short-lived, and the result of a recent surfeit or scarcity of sales in a particular market.

■ A Japanese Foreign Ministry official, who briefed reporters Wednesday, said Tokyo did not want to discuss "short-term _____ in exchange rates."

The best word for this group of sentences is

_____.

commodity distribution indication	**5.** ■ This type of generalization requires the comparison of maps showing the two spatial patterns of elevation of the terrain above sea-level and the _____ of pine trees over that same terrain. ■ Food processing, packaging, and pharmaceuticals are also important. The town has also become an important _____ center, thanks to its location, with excellent access to the highway, the airport, and the east coast ports. ■ As a result of an investigation which found evidence of plagiarism, the publisher announced yesterday that it is suspending sales and _____ of the book. **The best word for this group of sentences is** _____ .

WEB POWER

You will find additional exercises related to the content in this chapter at **http://esl.college.hmco.com/students.**

Success in College

In this chapter, you will

- Become familiar with twenty-four high-frequency academic English words
- Examine the range of meanings of academic words
- Read about multiple intelligences
- Examine attitudes of commitment and persistence in university life

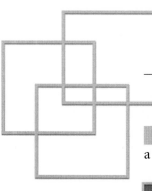

Section 1

EXERCISE 1 For each bold vocabulary word in Word List 2.1, write a short definition. Read the examples, and use a dictionary if necessary.

WORD LIST 2.1	
Word/Examples	**Definitions**
colleague (*n.*) . . . some of my *colleagues* in other departments . . .	
differentiate (*v.*) This study *differentiates* between three types of risk.	
distort (*v.*) The new policy may *distort* prices.	
empirical (*adj.*) . . . the *empirical* evidence suggests . . .	
insight (*n.*) . . . gain deeper *insight* into the human mind . . .	
nonetheless (*adv.*) The plot was inane, but you must admit, *nonetheless*, that the play was entertaining.	
predict (*v.*) Nobody could have *predicted* that the public mood would change so quickly.	
visual (*adj.*) . . . *visual* impact . . .	

EXERCISE 2 Before reading the following passage, answer this question.

Intelligence quotient (IQ) has been a form of measuring intelligence for over half a century. However, many now question the completeness of that measure. What kinds of intelligence might not be measured in a test of reading, writing, mathematics, and logic?

_____

_____

_____

Reading 1

GARDNER'S THEORY OF MULTIPLE INTELLIGENCES

Book learning is one kind of intelligence, but is it the only kind? While some researchers believe intelligence is a single ability measured by IQ tests, others **differentiate** between various types of intelligence. Howard Gardner, a professor at Harvard University's Graduate School of Education, belongs to the second camp, arguing that intelligence includes eight **discrete** components. Everyone possesses these intelligences to varying degrees, but some people may show greater strength in one or more areas. Gardner also believes that we can encourage the development of our intelligences and that we can learn to use them to our advantage.

Linguistic. This intelligence is characterized by skill with words and sensitivity to their meanings, sounds, and functions. If your linguistic intelligence is high, you probably learn best by reading.

Logical-Mathematical. This intelligence is characterized by skill with numbers, scientific ability, and formal reasoning. If your logical-mathematical intelligence is high, you probably learn best by taking a problem-solving approach to learning. Outlining or making charts and graphs may be good study techniques for you.

Bodily-Kinesthetic. This intelligence enables people to use their bodies skillfully and in goal-oriented ways such as playing a sport or dancing. If your bodily intelligence is high, you may be able to learn more effectively by combining study with some physical activity.

Musical. This intelligence is characterized by the ability to find meaning in music and other rhythmical sounds and to reproduce them either vocally or with an instrument. If your musical intelligence is high, you may want to choose a career in music or engage in leisure activities that allow you to pursue your musical interests. Although studying to music is a distraction for some, you may find that it aids your concentration.

Spatial. This intelligence is characterized by the ability to perceive the world accurately and to mentally reorganize or reinterpret those perceptions. For example, an artist perceives accurately what a bowl of fruit looks like, but the artist's representation is a new interpretation—the artist's mental image of the bowl of fruit, which may **distort** the shapes and sizes or change the colors of the fruit. If your spatial intelligence is high, you may learn best by finding ways to **visualize** or restructure the material that you want to learn.

Interpersonal. This intelligence is characterized by the ability to read people's moods and intentions and to have **insights** into what drives their motivation. People who have a high degree of interpersonal intelligence may be said to have "good people skills." If your interpersonal intelligence is high, you may learn best by collaborating with **colleagues** on projects or by participating in a study group.

Intrapersonal. This intelligence is characterized by self-knowledge: the ability to read your own emotions, to understand what motivates you, and to use that understanding to shape your behavior. If your intrapersonal intelligence is high, you should be able to use all your other intelligences to find the best study methods that will work for you.

Naturalistic. This intelligence is the ability to perceive the world from an environmental perspective: feeling, sensing, and relating to your environment through its natural features and rhythms. For example, people living in remote cultures become skilled at coping with nature, navigating without maps, and surviving in a hostile climate. For others, this intelligence may reveal itself in curiosity about nature, love of the outdoors, or special ability in the natural sciences.

Gardner's theory of multiple intelligences (MI) is widely accepted among educators. **Nonetheless**, opinions about the theory's usefulness differ. Some psychologists and educators praise Gardner for raising public awareness about the various facets of intellectual ability, but others are concerned because there is no **empirical** research to support the theory. Most employers place great value on verbal and math skills, believing that they may possibly **predict** success at work. The practical value of Gardner's theory may be that it encourages students to discover and use all of their talents and intellectual capabilities to create success in college and in life.

Source: Kanar, C. (2004). *The Confident Student.* Boston: Houghton Mifflin, pp. 36–37.

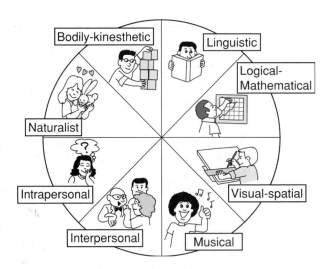

EXERCISE **3** Answer the following questions based on Reading 1. In your answers, try to use the vocabulary words given in parentheses.

1. Why do you think standard IQ was not sufficient to explain intelligence? (*differentiate*)

_____

_____

_____

2. Choose two intelligences as the best <u>predictors</u> for each of these careers: lawyer, physician, computer programmer, baseball player. Write your choices in the chart. On the lines, explain your choices.

_____

_____

_____

Lawyer		
Physician		
Computer programmer		
Baseball player		

EXERCISE 4   Notice how these verbs from Chapter 1 form nouns:

accumulate ⟶ accumulation
fluctuate ⟶ fluctuation
perceive ⟶ perception
exploit ⟶ exploitation

All the verbs below can be made into nouns by using a suffix ending in -ion. Complete the chart by writing a noun for each verb. Use a dictionary to check your work.

Verb		Noun
differentiate	⟶	
distort	⟶	
visualize	⟶	
predict	⟶	

Master Student Tip

Suffixes are important indicators of a word's part of speech. For example, the suffixes *-tion* and *-sion* usually show that a word is a noun and that the word is an action or idea (rather than a person or an object). When you see words having the same suffixes, try to determine if that suffix follows a part-of-speech pattern like *-tion* and *-sion*.

EXERCISE 5 It is important to use different word forms when rephrasing ideas represented by academic words. Review each excerpt from Reading 1. Then, complete its rephrased sentence by writing a different word form of the bold vocabulary word. In the parentheses, write the part of speech of the new word form. The first one has been done for you as an example.

1. "While some researchers believe intelligence is a single ability measured by IQ tests, others **differentiate** between various types of intelligence."

   Some researchers believe in measuring intelligence by using IQ tests; however, others believe that _differentiation (noun)_ between various types of intelligence is important.

2. "Some people have **insights** into what drives motivation."

   Some people are very _____ (_____) about what drives motivation.

3. "Some scientists are concerned because there is no **empirical** research to support the theory."

   Some scientists are concerned because there is little to support the theory _____ (_____).

4. "Most employers believe verbal and math skills can **predict** success at work."

   Most employers believe verbal and math skills are stronger _____ (_____) of success at work.

5. "The artist's representation of a bowl of fruit may **distort** the shapes and sizes or change the colors of the fruit."

   The artist's representation of a bowl of fruit may produce _____ (_____) in shape and size or changes in color.

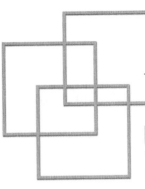

Section 2

EXERCISE 6 For each bold vocabulary word in Word List 2.2, write a short definition. Look at the example phrases and sentences, and use a dictionary if necessary.

WORD LIST 2.2

Word/Examples	Definitions
attain (*v.*) Hard work helped them *attain* their objectives.	
facilitate (*v.*) Increased funding will *facilitate* the construction of new infrastructure.	
likewise (*adv.*) Their budget has been cut, and we will *likewise* have to cut back on spending.	
ongoing (*adj.*) The protests against new construction are *ongoing*.	
persist (*v.*) Poverty and unemployment will *persist* if special measures are not taken.	
sustain (*v.*) Only a strong recovery could *sustain* a tax cut of that enormity.	
team (*n.*) . . . a *team* player . . .	
utilize (*v.*) We need to *utilize* every possible advantage.	

EXERCISE 7 Before reading the following passage, answer these questions.

1. What do you do to prepare to study? How do you utilize your study time?

_____

_____

2. Reading 2 discusses commitment and persistence. What do these terms mean to you?

_____

_____

Reading 2

ATTITUDES FOR STUDY

Reading and studying take time; there are no shortcuts, only efficient study techniques. To effectively **utilize** your study time, use proven strategies and develop the confidence-building attitudes of commitment and **persistence**. What are these attitudes and what do they have to do with studying?

Commitment—A commitment is a pledge. For example, in marriage two people pledge to love one another. **Likewise**, people who pledge money and time to support a cause are committed. In academic terms, an attitude of commitment means a willingness to pledge your time and effort to reach your goals. For example, if you are committed to success, then you will adopt the behaviors that **facilitate** success, such as regular attendance, sufficient preparation, and studying. Commitment also involves desire. Therefore, if you know what you want and how to get it, and you are willing to set goals, then you have the attitude of commitment.

Persistence—**Persistence** is the willingness to **sustain** effort over time, even in the face of difficulty. Remember when you learned to ride a bicycle or drive a car? These skills took time to master. But no matter how many times you fell off the bike or how many times you had to practice parking and backing up the car, finally you learned to ride or drive. Finally, you got your license. That took persistence. Moreover, you were committed to learn because you desired having those skills and the freedom they would give you. In academic terms, an attitude of persistence means a willingness to try out new strategies and to practice new skills as often as necessary until mastery is achieved. Persistence means not giving up in the face of failure but instead analyzing your mistakes to see what went wrong, then trying again. Through commitment and persistence, you can take control of your learning.

The attitudes of commitment and persistence also have a workplace connection. Having an <u>ongoing</u> commitment to a company's goals and being persistent in your efforts to <u>attain</u> them make you a valued employee. Further, you will be <u>perceived</u> as a **team** player who is willing to go the extra mile to reach common company goals.

Source: Kanar, C. (2004). *The Confident Student.* Boston: Houghton Mifflin, pp. 225–226.

EXERCISE **8** Answer the following questions based on Reading 2. In your answers, try to use the vocabulary words given in the parentheses.

1. In Reading 2, the author gives examples of commitment in marriage and in supporting causes. Write a paragraph about an experience when your commitment (or the commitment of someone you know) helped you (or her or him) succeed in a difficult situation. (*facilitate, sustain*)

_____

_____

_____

_____

2. The author mentions using strategies to build an attitude of commitment and <u>persistence</u>. What might some of those strategies be? (*utilize, likewise, ongoing*)

_____

_____

_____

_____

EXERCISE 9 Many words have multiple meanings. When using a dictionary to build your vocabulary, read all the meanings of an entry, not just the first one. Examine the following meanings of *sustain*. Then write the number of the meaning that best matches how the bold word is used in each sentence. One has been done for you as an example.

Meaning	Sentence
sustain (*v.*) [*tr.v.*]	

1. To keep something in existence, to maintain

2. To keep something or somebody alive by supplying needed nourishment

3. To support something from below, to keep it from falling or sinking

4. To support somebody's spirit

5. To experience or suffer (*usually injuries*)

_____ **A.** The cement-and-steel structure **sustained** the heavy weight of the building's upper floors.

_____ **B.** Perhaps your religious faith will **sustain** you through this ordeal.

___5__ **C.** Several key players **sustained** injuries in preseason training.

_____ **D.** Part of the challenge is treating the planet better so that we can **sustain** our children and their children; it is about our survival as a competitive and wealthy nation.

_____ **E.** The administration believes that the president's plan has led to a situation that has **sustained** economic growth, with low inflation and low inflationary pressure.

Master Student Tip

Many English words have more than one meaning. When you read, you may see a word you know but it appears to be in the wrong context. That may mean a different meaning is being used. When you learn a word, find out if it has more than one meaning and what those meanings are.

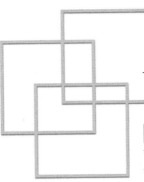

Section 3

EXERCISE 10 For each bold vocabulary word in Word List 2.3, write a short definition. Read the example sentences, and discuss the words with your classmates. Use a dictionary to check your work.

WORD LIST 2.3

Word/Examples	Definitions
convince (*v.*) She *convinced* us that she was right.	
deviate (*v.*) We *deviated* from our original strategy when it became clear that it wasn't working.	
encounter (*v.*) The conditions he *encountered* in those countries appear to have left a deep impression.	
initiate (*v.*) The Justice Department *initiated* an investigation of alleged wrongdoing by government contractors.	
reinforce (*v.*) Their bad behavior only *reinforced* his poor opinion of them.	
reluctance (*n.*) She showed great *reluctance* to criticize any part of the great artist's work.	
thereby (*adv.*) He filed divorce papers, *thereby* cutting off any chance of reconciliation.	
valid (*adj.*) The results are *valid*, but only for that specific population.	

EXERCISE 11 Before reading the following passage, answer these questions.

1. Do you think you are persistent enough now? Why or why not?

_____

_____

2. What might you change about yourself to become more persistent?

_____

_____

Reading 3

SEVEN SUGGESTIONS FOR BUILDING COMMITMENT AND PERSISTENCE

How do we go about building an attitude of commitment and persistence? Here are some suggestions:

- Choose success. **Convince** yourself that you will succeed.
- Be self-motivated. Think about why you are in college. Look to the future. Where do you want to be in five years? What is your dream job or career? Let your desires be your motivators.
- Set goals. Dreams don't come true without planning and effort. Set long-term goals (complete requirements for my major), set short-term goals (attain a 3.0 GPA this semester; earn an A on this assignment), and make plans to reach them. Commit yourself to the plans and try not to **deviate** from them—follow through!
- Remember that each day, each assignment, or each test brings you closer to achieving your goals. Make them all count. Put forth your best effort.
- Try out the strategies that you are learning. They won't do you any good if you read about them and then forget about them. For any study system to work, you have to **reinforce** it through consistent use, until it becomes second nature. Likewise, making organizers is an active process that involves you in learning. The value of both of these methods

is that they involve all your concentration, **thereby** making it less likely that a part of your brain will be on vacation while you are attempting to study.

- Don't give up. Suppose you have made a bad grade, or you think that you aren't making progress. Perhaps more practice is needed, or perhaps you need to try a new strategy. It's perfectly **valid** to seek help; above all, be persistent.

- Turn to your learning community. You are not alone. Don't be **reluctant** to talk to other students; they are likely to be **encountering** the same successes and failures that you are. **Initiate** contact with other concerned students to form a study group, and find out what works and doesn't work for them. Then revise your plans or methods as needed. Remember, you are in control.

Source: Kanar, C. (2004). *The Confident Student*. Boston: Houghton Mifflin, p. 226.

EXERCISE 12 Answer the following questions based on Reading 3. In your answers, try to use the vocabulary words given in the parentheses.

1. Do you think the suggestions are valid? Which do you think are most useful? Which do you think are not useful? Why? (*valid*)

_____

_____

_____

_____

2. What are some strategies you could use to convince yourself to succeed? Why might someone be reluctant to try these strategies? (*convince, reluctant*)

_____

_____

_____

_____

> **Master Student Tip**
>
> A prefix is added to the front of a word or word stem to change the meaning. One common prefix is *re-*, as in *reinforce*. This prefix can often mean "again" (e.g., *reread, reelect*), but it can also mean "backward" (e.g., *react, rewind, remove*). Understanding prefixes is useful when you encounter an unknown word, but it is also important to remember that the letters of a prefix (*re-*) may also start a word yet not affect its meaning (e.g., *reluctance, refine*).

EXERCISE 13 Write stress patterns for the following words. The first one has been done for you as an example. If you are not sure of your answers, check in a dictionary. Practice saying the words out loud, emphasizing the stress patterns.

1. convince   (___2___ – ___2___)

2. deviate   (_____ – _____)

3. deviant   (_____ – _____)

4. encounter   (_____ – _____)

5. initiate   (_____ – _____)

6. reinforce   (_____ – _____)

7. reluctance   (_____ – _____)

8. valid   (_____ – _____)

9. conviction   (_____ – _____)

10. deviation   (_____ – _____)

11. thereby   (_____ – _____)

12. initiative   (_____ – _____)

13. reinforcement   (_____ – _____)

14. reluctantly   (_____ – _____)

15. validity   (_____ – _____)

16. validate   (_____ – _____)

EXERCISE 14 Match each bold vocabulary word with its lettered meaning. Write the correct letter on the line. One has already been done for you as an example.

1. _____ **valid**

2. __*a*__ to **convince**

3. _____ to **reinforce**

4. _____ to **deviate**

5. _____ **reluctance**

6. _____ to **initiate**

7. _____ to **encounter**

8. _____ **thereby**

a. To persuade someone

b. To begin something

c. Hesitation about doing something

d. To meet someone/something unexpectedly

e. Because of that

f. To move away from an original path or plan

g. Logical or convincing

h. To add to something to make it stronger

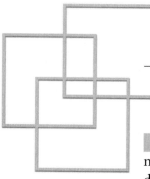

Section 4

CHAPTER 2 REVIEW

EXERCISE `15` Review the Chapter 2 Word List. Do you know the meaning(s) of each word? Do you know the part of speech? What different word forms do they have? How do you pronounce them?

attain	empirical	nonetheless	sustain
colleague	encounter	ongoing	team
convince	facilitate	persist	thereby
deviate	initiate	predict	utilize
differentiate	insight	reinforce	valid
distort	likewise	reluctance	visual

EXERCISE `16` Write the best word from the row to complete each sentence. You may have to change the word form (from the verb form to the adjective form, for example). Use a dictionary to check your work. The first one has been done for you as an example.

1. Wall Street is ___*convinced*___ that the Federal Reserve Board will cut short-term interest rates when it meets early next month.

    sustained   persistent   convinced   attainable

2. _____ is the willingness to sustain effort over time, even in the face of difficulty.

    distortion   insight   conviction   persistence

3. It is disturbing how his former friends and _____ in the department no longer acknowledge his work.

    team   colleagues   facilitators   deviants

4. He has such a large vocabulary that he can _____ between slightly different meanings without having to use any qualifying words.

    initiate   encounter   utilize   differentiate

5. The U.S. government has signaled its intention to maintain a presence in the area and is encouraging its allies to do _____.

    likewise   thereby   nonetheless   ongoing

6. She is _____ to speak publicly and risk losing her job.

    reluctant   empirical   valid   visual

7. It is still hard to _____ when the project will be finished.

    predict   reinforce   facilitate   validate

8. Those comments are so _____; it's almost as if she had been there during the process.

    insightful   ongoing   valid   distorted

WEB POWER

You will find additional exercises related to the content in this chapter at **http://esl.college.hmco.com/students.**

Social Psychology

In this chapter, you will

- Become familiar with twenty-three high-frequency academic English words
- Examine the eight key ways to build vocabulary
- Practice looking at words in context and noticing patterns
- Read about issues in social psychology

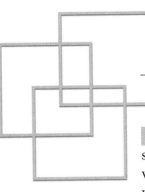

Section 1

EXERCISE 1 Look at the words and the example phrases and sentences in Word List 3.1. Put a check mark in the box next to each bold vocabulary word you already know. Write the part of speech for each word. You may use the examples to help determine the part of speech.

WORD LIST 3.1

Know it?	Word	POS	Example phrases/sentences
☐	adjacent		. . . move to an *adjacent* site . . . . . . an *adjacent* office . . .
☐	appendix		. . . a list of websites in an *appendix* . . . . . refer to *Appendix* A for a full report . . .
☐	commence		. . . activities *commence* at 3 p.m. . . . . . . to *commence* immediately . . .
☐	concurrently		. . . two sentences, to be served *concurrently* . . . . . . held two positions *concurrently* . . .
☐	discrete		. . . *discrete* bits and pieces . . . . . . learned that again these are not *discrete* categories . . . . . . studied as *discrete* units . . .
☐	inclination		. . . they've shown little *inclination* to negotiate . . . . . . my personal *inclination* is to . . .
☐	straightforward		. . . it seemed so *straightforward* and simple . . . . . . simply a *straightforward* matter of . . .
☐	supplement		. . . she needs to *supplement* her income . . . . . . intended to *supplement* earlier information . . .

EXERCISE 2   Before reading the following passage, answer these questions.

1. What is your attitude toward sport utility vehicles (SUVs)?

_____

_____

2. What reasons would you give to either buy or not buy an SUV?

_____

_____

Reading 1

SOCIAL PSYCHOLOGY: ATTITUDES

What are your attitudes toward gun control laws, sport utility vehicles (SUVs), and vegetarian diets? An attitude is the evaluation or judgment of an object, person, or social issue. Social psychologists conceptualize attitudes as consisting of three components that occur **concurrently**: (1) cognition (sets of beliefs), (2) emotions (feelings of liking or disliking), and (3) behaviors (**inclinations** to act positively or negatively). The importance we give to attitudes is a function of their personal relevance. Our attitudes toward sport utility vehicles (love them, hate them) will be more important to us if we happen to be considering buying one. Yet research shows that the more often we express a particular attitude, the more important it is likely to become to us.

Sources of Attitudes. Our attitudes are acquired from many sources in our social environment—our parents, teachers, peers, personal experiences, and media sources. Not surprisingly, people from similar backgrounds tend to hold similar attitudes. Yet evidence also suggests that the attitude-building process may **commence** much earlier in life. Studies of twins raised separately show a surprising degree of shared attitudes on a number of **discrete** issues that cannot be explained by a common environmental influence. One hypothesis is that people do not inherit a gene for a particular attitude, but rather that heredity works in a less **straightforward** manner. It **supplements** environmental factors, influencing intelligence, temperaments, or personality traits that make people more or less likely to develop certain attitudes.

A link between behavior and attitude? Attitudes are not as closely linked to behavior as you might think. A person may hold favorable attitudes toward diversity in housing yet still refuse to purchase a home in areas in or **adjacent** to neighborhoods with diverse ethnic populations. Investigators find that attitudes, overall, are only modestly related to behavior. The lack of consistency between attitudes and behaviors reflects many factors, especially situational constraints. We may have an **inclination** to act in a certain way but be unable to carry out the action because of specific demands we face in that particular situation. Under some conditions, however, attitudes are more strongly linked to behavior—such as when the attitudes are more stable and held with a greater degree of confidence or certainty, when they relate specifically to the behavior at hand, and when they can be more readily recalled from memory.

Nevid, J. (2003). *Psychology Concepts and Applications.* Boston: Houghton Mifflin, pp. 629–630.

EXERCISE 3 Answer the following questions based on Reading 1. In your answers, try to use the vocabulary words given in parentheses.

1. How are behaviors defined in the reading? (*inclination*)

_____

_____

_____

2. At what age do you believe the formation of attitudes commences? (*commence*)

_____

_____

_____

Master Student Tip

There are eight main ways to build vocabulary knowledge:

1. Meaning (or multiple meanings)	The meanings a word has when used for communication, including its "core" or main meaning along with less common meanings and idiomatic usage
2. Spoken form	How to pronounce it
3. Written form	How to spell it
4. Frequency	How common the word is and whether it is used more or less frequently than its synonyms
5. Grammar of the word and its word forms	How the word fits into sentences, and how it can change for different parts of speech (different members of the word family)
6. Collocations	What the most likely words are that combine with the word, and the ways that those word combinations are most often used
7. Register	The way the word is restricted to specific situations, like its use in informal conversation or in formal academic writing
8. Associations the word has with other words and concepts	What categories the word belongs to, and its synonyms, antonyms, and other related words

EXERCISE 4 If you learn all eight ways to build vocabulary knowledge (see Master Student Tip), you will have an excellent start on your ability to use a word accurately and with confidence. These ways to build vocabulary knowledge are true for almost all kinds of words, especially academic words. Review the examples below, and then complete the grid. Write at least one way for each bold vocabulary word. Use a dictionary to help you make your "Notes" answers more complete. Compare your answers with your classmates'. Several answers have been done for you as examples.

Word	Way	Notes
appendix	meaning (#1)	Appendix can mean a body part or the extra section at the end of a book or article.
commence	register (#7)	This is a more formal word; a less formal word would be "start" or "begin."
	spoken form (#2)	Stress is on the 2nd syllable—comMENCE (compare with COMmerce)
adjacent		
concurrent		
discrete		
inclination		
straightforward		
supplement		

Master Student Tip

It's important to know the eight main ways of building vocabulary knowledge. It is also important for you to decide *which* ways are the best ones for you. Usually, if you want to write well using a word, you must know the last four ways of knowing a word (grammar, collocations, register, associations). Of the vocabulary words in Section 1, which ones do you think you will use in your writing more than the others? Why?

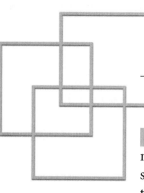

Section 2

EXERCISE 5 Study Word List 3.2. Put a check mark in the box next to each bold vocabulary word you already know. Write the part of speech for each word. Use the example sentences to help you determine the parts of speech.

WORD LIST 3.2

Know it?	Word	POS	Example sentences
☐	cease		The conversations *ceased* abruptly when she rose to speak.
☐	confine		Writers who work in a second language may have greater challenges than writers whose experience is *confined* to one language and culture.
☐	denote		The symbol $f(x)$ *denotes* the value of the function f at the element x.
☐	depressed		The news left him *depressed* and unable to see joy in any of his usual activities.
☐	forthcoming		Anticipation is high for the *forthcoming* book on human aggression, due out in several months.
☐	hypothesis		I believe that the results of the study are consistent with my *hypothesis*.
☐	qualitative		Our department does both *qualitative* and quantitative research.
☐	refined		The process will be *refined* during the next few years as more data are collected.

EXERCISE 6 Before reading the following passage, answer these questions.

1. What do you find attractive about your friends?

_____

_____

2. How are feelings towards friends different from romantic attraction?

_____

_____

Reading 2

SOCIAL PSYCHOLOGY: WHAT IS ATTRACTIVE?

In psychology, attraction is described as liking others as well as having positive thoughts about them and inclinations to act positively toward them. Though we usually think of attraction in terms of romantic or erotic attraction (attraction toward a love interest), social psychologists use the term more broadly to include other kinds of attraction as well, such as feelings of liking toward friends. There are four key determinants of attraction: similarity, proximity, reciprocity, and physical attractiveness.

We are generally attracted to people with whom we share similar attitudes. We also tend to like people who are similar to us in such characteristics as physical appearance, social class, race, height, musical tastes, and intelligence. The most widely held explanation for this is that similarity is gratifying because each person in the relationship serves to validate, reinforce, and enhance the other's self-concept. If you echo my sentiments about movies, politics, and the like, I might feel better about myself.

Friendship patterns are strongly influenced by physical proximity. For example, many casual friendships may **cease** once one or the other friend moves away. In classroom situations, Emily Ang might be more likely to become friends with Maria Arnez than with Sally Smith. Why? Because people whose last names begin with the same letter of the alphabet or an adjacent letter are more likely to be seated near each other and thus are more likely to form friendships.

Reciprocity is the tendency to like others who like us back. We typically respond well to people who compliment us or tell us how much they like us. Reciprocal interactions build upon themselves, leading to increased positive feelings on both sides. However, people often become distrustful if compliments are too **forthcoming**, or if people seem to show affection without the requisite time in intermediate stages of friendship. At that point, it becomes easy to think that someone wants something, or else is not very discriminating in choosing their friends.

We might think we are attracted romantically to people because of their inner qualities. However, **qualitative** evidence shows that it is the outer packaging, not the inner soul, that is the major determinant of initial attraction. People across cultures tend to view beauty in highly similar ways. Evidence suggests that the ideal female face varies little across cultures. Both men and women tend to judge the same faces as attractive; they also tend to agree that faces of women with more feminine features are more attractive than those with more masculine features. Yet perhaps surprisingly, in one study both male and female raters generally found male faces with more feminine features to be more attractive. The more **refined** and delicate features of a Leonardo DiCaprio, for example, are preferred over the more square-jawed, masculine features of an Arnold Schwarzenegger.

Although some features of physical beauty appear to be universal, cultural differences do exist. In certain African cultures, for example, feminine beauty is associated with physical features such as long necks and round, disk-like lips. Female plumpness **denotes** wealth and status in some societies, while in others, including most of U.S. society, the female ideal is associated with an unrealistic standard of thinness. Slenderness in men is also valued in Western society, but unrelenting social pressure to be thin is usually **confined** to women.

What happens if you don't happen to meet standards of physical perfection? Don't get too **depressed**. Only small relationships have been found between physical attractiveness and feelings of well-being. There is also the matching **hypothesis**, the prediction that people will seek partners who are similar to themselves in physical attractiveness. The matching **hypothesis** covers more than just perceived attractiveness; we tend to marry people who have similar personality traits, attitudes, and even body weight.

Nevid, J. (2003). Psychology Concepts and Applications. Boston: Houghton Mifflin, pp. 634–636.

EXERCISE 7 Discuss these questions about Reading 2 with other students. In your answers, try to use the vocabulary words given in the parentheses.

1. What denotes wealth and status in U.S. culture? Is it the same in other cultures? (*denote*)

_____

_____

2. What is the "matching hypothesis"? Do you think it is true? Why or why not? (*hypothesis*)

_____

_____

EXERCISE 8 Complete the chart by writing word forms from Word List 3.2 in the correct categories below. If you think a word fits into more than one category, list it more than once. The first one has been done for you as an example. Use a dictionary to check your work.

Nouns	Verbs	Adjectives	Adverbs
cessation	cease	ceaseless	ceaselessly
	confine		
	denote		
	depress		
		forthcoming	
hypothesis			
		qualitative	
	refine		

EXERCISE 9 Write stress patterns for the following words. The first one has been done for you as an example. After you are done, use a dictionary to check your work.

1. cease   (___/___ – ___/___)

2. depression   (_____ – _____)

3. forthcoming   (_____ – _____)

4. hypothesis   (_____ – _____)

5. qualitative   (_____ – _____)

6. refined   (_____ – _____)

7. ceaseless   (_____ – _____)

8. hypothetical   (_____ – _____)

9. qualitatively   (_____ – _____)

10. hypothesize   (_____ – _____)

11. denotation   (_____ – _____)

12. hypothetically   (_____ – _____)

Master Student Tip

Sometimes a word has both a literal and a figurative meaning. A literal meaning is one that is physical and concrete; a figurative meaning is a more abstract reference to the literal meaning. For example, *confine* can mean that something or someone is restricted to a specific location: *He was quite ill and confined to his bed.* It can also have a more figurative use: *The debate must be confined to the amendment being voted on.* This meaning still means that there is a boundary or restriction, but it is not a physical boundary.

When you are learning new words, it is useful to know if a word has both literal and figurative meanings. Use a dictionary to determine if the words *depress*, *confine*, and *refine* in this chapter have both literal and figurative meanings. Discuss their meanings with a group of classmates.

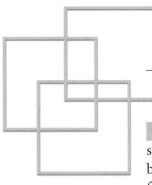

Section 3

EXERCISE 10 Look at the words and the example phrases and sentences in Word List 3.3. Put a check mark in the box next to each bold vocabulary word you already know. Write the part of speech for each word. You may use the examples to help determine the part of speech.

<table>
<tr><td colspan="4">**W O R D   L I S T   3 . 3**</td></tr>
<tr><th>Know it?</th><th>Word</th><th>POS</th><th>Example phrase/sentence</th></tr>
<tr><td>☐</td><td>**amendment**</td><td></td><td>. . . a constitutional *amendment* . . .</td></tr>
<tr><td>☐</td><td>**intermediate**</td><td></td><td>The second round of interviews is essentially an *intermediate* stage in research.</td></tr>
<tr><td>☐</td><td>**mediate**</td><td></td><td>. . . Mubarak has been *mediating* between the two sides.</td></tr>
<tr><td>☐</td><td>**protocol**</td><td></td><td>. . . a serious breach of *protocol* . . .</td></tr>
<tr><td>☐</td><td>**revolution**</td><td></td><td>. . . years of war, *revolution*, and suppression . . .</td></tr>
<tr><td>☐</td><td>**suspend**</td><td></td><td>. . . lights *suspended* in the trees . . .</td></tr>
<tr><td>☐</td><td>**terminate**</td><td></td><td>. . . we must *terminate* the contract if they do not pay on time . . .</td></tr>
</table>

EXERCISE 11 Before reading the following passage, answer these questions.

1. What do you do when you feel angry?

_____

_____

_____

_____

2. Can you recall a time when you acted aggressively? What prompted this behavior?

_____

_____

_____

_____

Reading 3

SOCIAL PSYCHOLOGY: HUMAN AGGRESSION

Far too often in human history negative attitudes toward members of other groups have set the stage for violent behavior in the form of killing, warfare, and violent **revolution**. Many people believe that we have just concluded the bloodiest, most violent century in the history of humankind. It was a century marked not just by two major world wars that claimed millions of lives but also by countless armed conflicts between opposing countries and factions, some of which have not yet been **terminated**. We have witnessed wholesale slaughters of civilian populations in which human decency seemed to have been completely **suspended**, and outright genocide perpetuated on a scale unparalleled in human history.

What are we to make of all this? Are human beings inherently aggressive? Or is aggression a form of learned behavior that can be modified by experience? There are many opinions among psychologists and other scientists about the nature of human aggression. Let us consider what the major perspectives in psychology might teach us about our capacity to harm one another.

Some theorists have believed that aggression in humans and other species is based on instinct, and a basic survival mechanism in many animal species. Most contemporary theorists, however, believe that human aggression is far too complex to be based solely on instinct. A theory of human aggression based on instinct must be **amended** to account for this complexity. Major influences include biological, sociocultural, and emotional influences, as well as the significant **mediating** factors of alcohol and the environment.

One possible factor may be biological. In particular, the neurotransmitter serotonin and the male hormone testosterone may play an **intermediate** role in aggressive behavior. However, the evidence is not conclusive. For example, not all men with high levels of testosterone are excessively aggressive. Another factor might be learned habits and broader social contexts against which aggressive acts occur. Abused or neglected children often fail to develop an awareness of the rules and **protocol** of normal society and may display violent behaviors later in life. Another influence is emotion; certain negative emotions, such as frustration and anger, may trigger aggressive behavior. Frequently having these emotions may not necessarily result in violence, however, and can in fact trigger a positive reaction if an individual recognizes and deals with the emotion constructively.

Alcohol use, which lowers inhibitions on impulsive acts of violence, is strongly linked to aggressive behavior. It also lessens sensitivity to external cues and causes misreadings of possible outcomes to actions. However, a person's reaction to alcohol is **mediated** by many factors, both biological and cultural.

Environmental psychologists are investigating another potential factor in aggressive behavior—the physical surroundings in which a person lives. Findings suggest that higher temperatures can lead to more physical intimidation and threatening behavior. Should we consider turning up the air conditioning in our schools, offices, and prisons?

Nevid, J. (2003). *Psychology Concepts and Applications.* Boston: Houghton Mifflin. pp. 643–647.

EXERCISE 12 Answer these questions about Reading 3. In your answers, try to use the vocabulary words given in the parentheses.

1. Some might say that human aggression leads to violent revolution. Do you agree? In your opinion, what are the causes of violent revolution? (*revolution*)

_____

_____

_____

2. Protocol dictates how people should act in certain situations. Discuss situations in which you had to be aware of protocol (examples: going to court, attending a graduation, going to a religious ceremony). (*protocol*)

_____

_____

_____

EXERCISE 13 Complete the word fragments below. On each line write a different word form from vocabulary words in this section. Then write the part of speech and the stress pattern for each word you complete. The first one has been done for you as an example.

1. amen_____

   a. ____amendment____ (_____noun_____) (___3___ – ___2___)

   b. _____amend_____ (_____verb_____) (___2___ – ___1___)

   c. _____amended_____ (__past tense verb__) (___3___ – ___2___)

2. suspen_____

   a. _____ (_____) (_____ – _____)

   b. _____ (_____) (_____ – _____)

   c. _____ (_____) (_____ – _____)

3. termin_____

    a. _____ (_____) (_____ – _____)

    b. _____ (_____) (_____ – _____)

    c. _____ (_____) (_____ – _____)

4. revol_____

    a. _____ (_____) (_____ – _____)

    b. _____ (_____) (_____ – _____)

    c. _____ (_____) (_____ – _____)

EXERCISE 14 Write words from the word bank that answer these questions.

amend	intermediate	protocol	revolution	suspend	terminate

1. _____ Which word is usually used to talk about changing a law?

2. _____ Which word, in this form, can be either a noun or an adjective?

3. _____ Which word often uses adjectives like *royal*, *strict*, and *legal*?

4. _____ Which word has the same pronunciation stress pattern as termination?

5. _____; _____ Which two words have three syllables and have the first syllable stressed?

6. _____ Which word is the most difficult for you to pronounce? Be ready to discuss how to work on this.

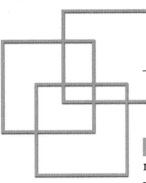

Section 4

CHAPTER 3 REVIEW

EXERCISE 15 Review the Chapter 3 Word List. Do you know the meaning of each word? Do you know the part of speech? What different word forms do they have?

adjacent	confine	incline	revolution
amend	denote	intermediate	straightforward
append	depress	mediate	supplement
cease	discrete	protocol	suspend
commence	forthcoming	qualitative	terminate
concurrently	hypothesis	refine	

EXERCISE 16 Write each word from the Chapter 3 Word List in the correct box for its pronunciation pattern. Two have been done for you as examples.

2–1	3–1	4–1
incline		
2–2		**4–2**
amend		
		4–3

	3–2	
		5–3

EXERCISE 17 Change the following words into other forms. The first one has been done for you as an example. Use a dictionary to check your work.

commence	verb ⟶ noun	*commencemnt*
supplement	noun ⟶ adjective	
revolution	noun ⟶ adjective	
hypothesis	noun ⟶ adjective	
confine	verb ⟶ noun	
depress	verb ⟶ adjective	
mediate	verb ⟶ noun	
terminate	verb ⟶ noun	

W E B   P O W E R

You will find additional exercises related to the content in this chapter at **http://esl.college.hmco.com/students**

Ethics

In this chapter, you will

- Become familiar with twenty-five high-frequency academic English words
- Learn how to look at concordance lines for vocabulary words
- Consider how and when to learn antonyms
- Read about several issues in the study of ethics

Section 1

EXERCISE 1 For each bold vocabulary word in Word List 4.1, write a short definition. Read the examples, and use a dictionary to check your work.

WORD LIST 4.1

Word/Examples	Definition

albeit (*conj.*)
She has a sense of humor, *albeit* a bizarre one.
Profits are increasing, *albeit* at a pace much
slower than projected.

ambiguous (*adj.*)
The answers I received were somewhat *ambiguous*.
. . . unclear and *ambiguous* guidelines . . .

analogous (*adj.*)
. . . a mission *analogous* to that of an army in
combat . . .
certain organisms were considered *analogous* to
man-made machines.

conversely (*adj.*)
A millionaire through inheritance is not in the same
social class as someone who is poverty-stricken with
no economically meaningful skills. *Conversely*, a
surgeon and an engineer may be in the same social
class though their skills are quite different.

complement (*v.*)
With their separate ambitions, they actually
complement each other quite well.
This new research was intended to *complement*
her earlier work.

Word/Examples	Definition

ethical (*adj.*)
...the debate on *ethical* and moral issues ...
...*ethical* behavior ...
...*ethical* dilemma ...
...he refused on *ethical* grounds ...

norms (*pl.n.*)
...principles and *norms* of equity and service ...
...*norms* of behavior ...
...cultural/traditional/social *norms* ...

passive (*adj.*)
Active and *passive* actually apply to how students
are learning.
The problem is that we are preparing students
to be *passive* learners, but when they enter
professional programs they are asked to be
active learners.

violation (*n.*)
The incident was a serious *violation* of the
Geneva Convention.
...a *violation* of her civil rights ...
Their actions were in *violation* of the
U.S. Constitution.

EXERCISE 2 Before reading the following passage, answer these
questions.

1. Look at the first few lines of Reading 1. Which of the listed statements
   do you think most accurately describes ethics?

   _____

   _____

2. Write your own definition of ethics.

   _____

   _____

Reading 1

What Is Ethics?

A few years ago, sociologist Raymond Baumhart asked people, "What does **ethics** mean to you?" Among their replies were the following:

> "Ethics has to do with what my feelings tell me is right or wrong."
> "Ethics has to do with my religious beliefs."
> "Being **ethical** is doing what the law requires."
> "Ethics consists of the standards of behavior our society accepts."
> "I don't know what the word means."

The meaning of "ethics" can seem **ambiguous**, and the views many people have about ethics are shaky. Like Baumhart's first respondent, many people tend to see ethics as **analogous** to feelings. However, being ethical is clearly not a matter of merely following one's feelings. A person following his or her feelings may recoil from doing what is right. In fact, what a person feels frequently deviates sharply from what is ethical.

Nor should one identify ethics with religion. Most religions, of course, advocate high ethical standards. Yet if ethics were confined to religion, then ethics would apply only to religious people. Yet an atheist or agnostic can maintain high ethical standards, **albeit** outside the realm of the traditionally religious. **Conversely**, a deeply religious person might engage in unethical behavior. Religion can set high ethical standards and can provide intense motivations for ethical behavior, yet ethics cannot be confined to religion nor is it the same as religion.

Being ethical is also not the same as **passively** following the law. The law often incorporates ethical standards to which most citizens subscribe. But laws, like feelings, can deviate from what is ethical. Our own pre-Civil War slavery laws and the apartheid laws once held in South Africa are grotesquely obvious examples of laws that **violate** what we view as ethical.

Finally, being ethical is not the same as following societal **norms**, or doing "whatever society accepts." In any society, most people accept standards that are, in fact, ethical. But standards of behavior in society can deviate from what is ethical, as shown in the example of U.S. slavery laws before the Civil War. Moreover, if being ethical were doing "whatever society accepts," then to find out what is ethical, one would have to find out what society accepts. No one ever tries to decide an ethical issue by doing a survey. Further, the lack of social consensus on many issues makes it impossible to equate ethics with whatever society accepts. If being ethical were doing whatever society accepts, one would have to find an agreement on issues, such as abortion or same-sex marriage, which does not, in fact, exist.

What, then, is ethics? Ethics has two components that **complement** each other. First, ethics refers to standards of right and wrong that govern what humans ought to do, usually in terms of rights, obligations, benefits to society, fairness, or specific virtues supported by consistent and well-founded reasons. Second, ethics refers to the study and development of one's own ethical standards. Ethics also means, then, the continuous studying of our own moral beliefs and our moral conduct, and striving to ensure that we, and the institutions we help to shape, live up to standards that are reasonable and solidly-based.

Source: Markkula Center for Applied Ethics. (2004). *What Is Ethics?* http://www.scu.edu/ethics/practicing/decision/whatisethics.html.

EXERCISE   3   Answer the following questions based on Reading 1. In your answers, try to use the vocabulary words given in the parentheses.

1. Why might the author consider ethics to be an **ambiguous** area? Give examples of issues in which **ethical** behavior is not clearly distinguished from unethical behavior. (*ambiguous, ethical, unethical*)

_____

_____

_____

_____

2. What societal **norms**, either in the United States or in another culture, do you believe violate your own **ethical** standards? How should we deal with societal norms that we do not agree with? Discuss your answers. (*ethical, norms, violation*)

_____

_____

_____

_____

Master Student Tip

What is a concordance? A concordance is a list of example sentences that contain a specific word, called the *target word*. These example sentences are taken from various authentic writing or speaking sources, and this authenticity allows you to see how the target word is used in real situations. Concordances can be useful to you when learning about academic vocabulary because you can see what words often go together, as well as the common grammatical structures a word is in.

Look at these concordance lines for *enormous*. *Influence, potential,* and *sums* combine with *enormous*. Only one line uses *enormous* to describe something that is physically large (eyes). This word-combination information may not be in every dictionary, but it is important knowledge that native speakers have (and that you need in order to speak and write in a fluent, effective style).

```
      playwrights and me included do an  enormous  amount of rewriting in
  example, Helen Shapiro had had four  enormous  hits several with a
     has, obviously, countrywide, has an  enormous  impact on the economy.
   making it hard to leave. He had an  enormous  influence on United when
      a fraud. Dawn said:"They went to  enormous  lengths to catch her out."
       has begun to realize some of its  enormous  potential for application
        This significant increase has put  enormous  pressure on the
         it means Japanese exporters have  enormous  sums of dollars they must
     We think nothing of handing over  enormous  sums of money to be
Those clinicians who function under  enormous  time pressures and have
     would it be?" Susanne's eyes were  enormous. What will it do to you?"
```

To find out how to get concordance lines on your own, go to our website and follow the links for *concordances*.

EXERCISE **4** Use the following concordance lines to answer questions about each bold vocabulary word.

		albeit	
1.	there was a wind,	albeit	a gentle one, from
2.	useful to consider,	albeit	briefly, the body's
3.	immediately arrested,	albeit	briefly. I was
4.	poses a direct,	albeit	little known, threat
5.	Right had a coherent,	albeit	nostalgic, vision of
6.	minute". A blessing,	albeit	put off for a week,
7.	see. There is a link,	albeit	tenuous, and in due
8.	go up and down stairs—	albeit	with unsubtle grace,

1. What kind of word or phrase follows *albeit*—noun, verb, adjective, or adverb?

_____

2. What punctuation usually comes right before *albeit*?

_____

3. When the word *albeit* is used, it typically introduces information that modifies the idea or word that comes before it. In the following examples, what modifying information is introduced by the word *albeit*?

■ What kind of wind? (line 1)

_____ *A gentle wind, which is weaker than expected* _____

■ How long was it considered? (line 2) _____

■ How long was he or she under arrest? (line 3) _____

■ How is the coherent vision described? (line 5) _____

■ What kind of link was it? (line 7) _____

■ How did the person go up and down stairs? (line 8) _____

4. Do you think that *albeit* makes the idea expressed stronger or weaker? Why?

_____

_____

	analogous	
1.	to see the Net as	analogous	to cable TV
2.	their lessons. It is	analogous	to a father with
3.	The situation is	analogous	to a person who
4.	The process is	analogous	to an aggregation
5.	life. This value is	analogous	to beliefs about
6.	antiwar movement in	analogous	ways. But only the
7.	plant. The water is	analogous	to electricity in
8.	Well it's really	analogous	to looking for a
9.	Their position is	analogous	to that of France
10.	Addiction is	analogous	to the process of

1. What word usually follows *analogous*?

_____

2. Which words (nouns, verbs, etc.) are compared by using *analogous*?

_____

_____

3. List five of the pairs of ideas or words compared in the sentences indicated in the chart. The first one has been done for you as an example.

Sentence 1	Net	Cable TV
Sentence 5		
Sentence 7		
Sentence 9		
Sentence 10		

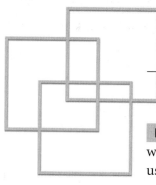

Section 2

EXERCISE 5 For each bold vocabulary word in Word List 4.2, write a short definition. Read the example phrases and sentences, and use a dictionary if necessary.

WORD LIST 4.2

Word/Examples	Definition
alter (*v.*) We *altered* our vacation plans at the last minute. The election could *alter* the balance of power in Washington	
comprise (*v.*) The French squad *comprised* 16 players. The committee should *comprise* six government representatives.	
conceive (*v.*) ... outraged over the ill-*conceived* plan ... Bakun Dam was *conceived* as the centerpiece for Malaysia's ambition to become a regional electricity powerhouse.	
infer (*v.*) ... cannot be proved directly, so it must be *inferred* from facts available ... You cannot *infer* from a high test score that a student has good computation skills.	
levy (*v.*) ... a huge fine *levied* against the company for polluting the river ... The tax would only be *levied* on imports.	

Word/Examples	Definition
minimal (*adj.*) ...damage was *minimal* when compared to the enormity of the 'explosion ... ...*minimal* planning ...	
mutual (*adj.*) ... by *mutual* agreement ... ... in our *mutual* interest ... ... they show *mutual* respect for one another ...	
whereby (*conj.*) ...a system *whereby* you can control input and output ... ... to try to develop a process *whereby* we can engage with the leadership to ... ...the agreement *whereby* decisions are made ...	

EXERCISE 6 Before reading the following passage, answer these questions.

1. What is "the common good"?

_____

_____

_____

2. Can you think of any situations in which your own interests were in conflict with the interests of a larger group (like the community or country)? Describe what happened.

_____

_____

_____

Reading 2

THE COMMON GOOD: ETHICS IN SOCIETY

Appeals to the common good have surfaced in discussions of business' social responsibilities, environmental pollution, our lack of investment in education, and the problems of crime and poverty. Everywhere, it seems, social commentators are claiming that our most fundamental social problems grow out of a widespread pursuit of individual interests.

What exactly is "the common good," and why has it come to have such a critical place in current discussions of problems in our society? The contemporary ethicist John Rawls defined the common good as "certain general conditions that are . . . equally to everyone's advantage." Examples of parts of the common good include an accessible and affordable public health care system, an effective system of public safety and security, peace among the nations of the world, a just legal and political system, an unpolluted natural environment, and a flourishing economic system with an equitable **levying** of taxes. It is no surprise that virtually every social problem in one way or another is linked to how well these systems and institutions are functioning.

As these examples suggest, the common good does not just happen. Establishing and maintaining the common good requires that people believe they have **mutual** interests and are willing to sacrifice for them. These sacrifices pay off, however, because the common good is a good to which all members of society have access, and from whose enjoyment no one can be easily excluded. In fact, something counts as a common good only to the extent **whereby** it is a good to which all have access.

It might be **inferred** that since all citizens benefit from the common good, we would all willingly cooperate in establishing and maintaining the common good. Nevertheless, numerous observers have identified a number of obstacles that hinder us, as a society, from successfully doing so.

First, according to some philosophers, the very idea of a common good is inconsistent with a pluralistic society like ours. Different people have different ideas about what is worthwhile or what constitutes "the good life for human beings." Given these differences, some people urge, it would be nearly **inconceivable** for us to agree on what particular kind of social systems, institutions, and environments we would all support.

A second problem encountered by proponents of the common good is what is sometimes called the "free-rider problem." The benefits that a common good provides are, as we noted, available to everyone, including those who choose not to do their part to maintain the common good. Individuals can become "free riders" by taking the benefits the common good provides while refusing to make even a **minimal** effort to support the common good. An adequate water supply, for example, is a common good, and during a drought, people must conserve water. Some individuals may be reluctant to **alter** their water usage, however, since they know that enough other people will conserve, and they can enjoy the benefits without reducing their own consumption. Many observers believe that this is what has happened to many of our common goods, such as the environment or education, where the reluctance of many people to support efforts to maintain these systems has led to their virtual collapse.

The third problem encountered by attempts to promote the common good is that of individualism. U.S. culture views society as **comprised** of separate independent individuals who are free to pursue their own individual goals and interests without interference from others. In this individualistic culture it is difficult, perhaps impossible, to convince people that they should sacrifice some of their freedom, some of their personal goals, and some of their self-interest, for the sake of the "common good." Our cultural traditions, in fact, reinforce the individual who thinks that she should not have to contribute to the community's common good, but should be left free to pursue her own personal ends.

Finally, appeals to the common good are confronted by the problem of an unequal sharing of burdens. Maintaining a common good often requires that particular individuals or particular groups bear costs that are much greater than those borne by others. Forcing particular groups or individuals to carry such unequal burdens "for the sake of the common good," is, arguably, unjust. Moreover, the prospect of having to carry such heavy and unequal burdens leads such groups and individuals to resist any attempts to secure common goods.

All of these problems pose considerable obstacles to those who call for an ethic of the common good. Still, appeals to the common good ought not to be dismissed, for they urge us to reflect on broad questions concerning the kind of society we want to become and how we are to achieve that society. They also challenge us to view ourselves as members of the same community and, while respecting and valuing the freedom of individuals to pursue their own goals, to recognize and further those goals we share in common.

Source: Markkula Center for Applied Ethics. (2004). *The Common Good.* http://www.scu.edu/ethics/practicing/decision/commongood.html

EXERCISE 7   Answer the following questions based on Reading 2. In your answers, try to use the vocabulary words given in the parentheses.

1. Governments levy taxes, and citizens pay them. Would you pay extra taxes if you believed that they would improve the common good, even if the improvement of your own situation was minimal? Why or why not? (*levy, minimal*)

_____

_____

_____

2. The people the author labels "free riders" refuse to make even a minimal effort to support the common good. They refuse to alter their lifestyle at all. What are some examples of this? Give reasons and possible solutions. (*minimal, alter*)

_____

_____

_____

EXERCISE 8   Complete the chart by writing word forms for each bold vocabulary word's part of speech. If no word form exists, write "none." After you are done, compare your answers with another student's. Then check in a dictionary for other forms of these words. The first one has been done for you as an example.

Noun	Verb	Adjective	Adverb
alternate alteration	**alter**	altered unaltered	none
	comprise		
	conceive		
	infer		
	levy		
		minimal	
		mutual	

Master Student Tip

Once you think you know a word well, try to find out how to express the opposite meaning (sometimes called antonyms). It can be more difficult learning two opposites together (like *left* and *right*; it is better to become familiar with *right* and then, later, work on *left*), so it is better to start working on opposite meanings after you have been practicing with the word. Once you know a word, such as ***ambiguous***, you can start working on its opposites.

Academic words usually have more than one way to express an opposite idea. For example, the opposite of *ambiguous* is *unambiguous*, but it can also be *clear*, *direct*, or *straightforward*, depending on the context. You can use a thesaurus to learn some words that have opposite meanings. Building your vocabulary means learning all the different ways to express the opposite idea. Choose three vocabulary words from Word List 4.2, and find their antonyms.

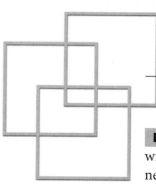

Section 3

EXERCISE **9** For each bold vocabulary word in Word List 4.3, write a short definition. Read the examples, and use a dictionary if necessary.

WORD LIST 4.3	
Word/Examples	**Definition**
aggregate (*n., adj.*) I don't have all the figures right in front of me, but the *aggregate* size is in the order of $45 million . . . . . . in the *aggregate* . . .	
assemble (*v.*) . . . a company that will *assemble*, manufacture, and sell vehicles . . . I need time to *assemble* a qualified group of experts.	
format (*n.*) The test is in the standard *format*. . . . the best *format* for the debate is in front of a live audience . . .	
integral (*adj.*) . . . he will play an *integral* role in our expansion plans . . . . . . it has become an *integral* part of everyday life . . .	
integrity (*n.*) . . . a serious lack of *integrity* . . . We need complete confidence in the *integrity* of the system	

Word/Examples	Definition
panel (*n.*) ...four-member *panel* ... ...a *panel* of experts ... ...an advisory *panel* ...	
paradigm (*n.*) ...a *paradigm* shift ... We should come up with a model, a new *paradigm*, that could be used in these types of situations.	
scenario (*n.*) ...a worst-case *scenario* ...	

EXERCISE 10   Before reading the following passage, answer these questions.

1. Have you ever had to make a difficult ethical decision? What was the situation? How did you feel about your decision at the time? How do you feel about it now?

_____

_____

_____

Reading 3

A FORMAT FOR ETHICAL DECISION MAKING

The field of ethics poses questions **integral** to how we ought to act and how we should live. It asks, "According to what standards are these actions right or wrong?" It asks, "What character traits (like **integrity**, compassion, fairness) are necessary to live a truly worthwhile life?" It also asks, "What concerns or groups do we usually minimize or ignore? And why might that be?" Admitting our blindness is the beginning of creating a new **paradigm** in which ethics can play a more prominent role.

Recognize a Moral Issue

- Is there something wrong personally, interpersonally, or socially? Is there conflict that could be damaging to people? to animals or the environment? to institutions? to society?
- Does the issue go deeper than legal or **institutional** concerns? What does it do to people as persons who have dignity, rights, and hopes for a better life together?

Assemble the Facts

- First, you need to compile all the relevant facts regarding the situation.
- What individuals and groups have an important stake in the outcome? What is at stake for each? Do some have a greater stake because they have a special need (e.g., those who are poor or excluded) or because we have special obligations to them? Are there other important stakeholders in addition to those directly involved?
- What are the options that you have envisioned to resolve the problem? Have all the relevant persons and groups been consulted? If you showed your list of options to a person you respect, what would that person say?

Evaluate the Alternative Scenarios from Various Moral Perspectives

- Which **scenario** will, in the **aggregate**, produce the most good and do the least harm?
- Which option respects the rights and dignity of all stakeholders? Even if not everyone gets all they want, will everyone still be treated fairly?
- Which option would promote the common good and help all participate more fully in the goods we share as a society, as a community, as a company, as a family?
- Which option would enable the deepening or development of those virtues or character traits that we value as individuals? as a profession? as a society?

Make a Decision

- Considering these perspectives, which of the options is the right thing to do?
- If you presented your decision to a **panel** of community or spiritual leaders whom you respected, what would their reaction be?

Act, Then Reflect on the Decision Later

How did it turn out for all concerned? If you had to do it over again, what, if anything, would you do differently?

Source: Markkula Center for Applied Ethics. (2004). *A Framework for Ethical Decision Making.* http://www.scu.edu/ethics/practicing/decision/framework.html

---

EXERCISE 11   Answer the following questions based on Reading 3. In your answers, try to use the vocabulary words given in the parentheses.

1. The author mentions that integrity is a character trait that many people believe to be important. When, if ever, might integrity be less important than other traits? (*integrity*)

   _____

   _____

   _____

   _____

2. If you had to choose people to be on a panel of community, business, and spiritual leaders, who would be on the panel? Whom would you exclude? Defend your choices. (*panel*)

   _____

   _____

   _____

   _____

Master Student Tip

Words usually are found with a certain group of other words. For example, if you are speaking or writing about *integrity*, it is likely that you will also use such vocabulary words as *character, morality,* and *ethics*. Knowing which words go together is an important part of building vocabulary knowledge.

EXERCISE **12** Write the vocabulary word from Word List 4.3 that best fits into each group. The first one has been done for you as an example.

1. build, put together, _assemble_

2. compassion, kindness, _____

3. total, entirety, _____

4. structure, shape, _____

5. connected, important, _____

6. group, experts, _____

7. view, perspective, _____

8. ideas, shift, _____

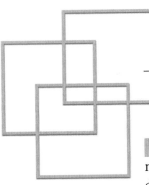

Section 4

CHAPTER 4 REVIEW

EXERCISE 13 Review the Chapter 4 Word List. Do you know the meaning(s) of each word? Do you know the part of speech? What different word forms do the words have? How do you pronounce them?

aggregate	comprise	integral	panel
albeit	conceive	integrity	paradigm
alter	converse	levy	passive
ambiguous	ethic	minimal	scenario
analogy	format	mutual	violated
assemble	infer	norm	whereby
complement			

EXERCISE 14 Change the following words into another form. The first one has been done for you as an example. Use a dictionary to check your work.

violation	noun to verb	_to violate_
paradigm	noun to adjective	_____
analogous	adjective to noun	_____
alter	verb to noun	_____
infer	verb to noun	_____
mutual	adjective to adverb	_____
conceive	verb to adjective	_____
ambiguous	adjective to noun	_____
conversely	adverb to adjective	_____
passive	adjective to noun	_____
ethical	adjective to adverb	_____
conceive	verb to noun	_____
complement	verb to adjective	_____

EXERCISE 15 Write what each group of words has in common. The common element can be based on meaning, suffixes, prefixes, pronunciation, or word forms. The first one has been done for you as an example.

1. aggregate   converse   levy

   All these words can be nouns or verbs.
   _____

2. unaltered   inconceivable   unambiguous

   _____

3. scenario   panel   paradigm

   _____

4. levy   format   ethic

   _____

5. comprise   conceive   converse

   _____

6. ethical   passive   analogous

   _____

7. integral   integrity   infer

   _____

8. albeit   assemble   comprising

   _____

W E B   P O W E R

You will find additional exercises related to the content in this chapter at **http://esl.college.hmco.com/students.**

Globalization

In this chapter, you will

- Become familiar with twenty-four high-frequency academic English words
- Use flash cards and vocabulary notebooks to build vocabulary knowledge
- Practice noticing register and the informal language that academic words can replace
- Consider issues related to globalization

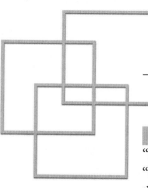

Section 1

EXERCISE **1** Look at Word List 5.1. Put a check mark in the "Know it?" box for each bold vocabulary word you already know. In each "Collocations" box, write any words you think are frequently used with the target word. The first one has been done for you as an example.

WORD LIST 5.1

Know it?	Collocations (list these)	Targt word	Part of speech	Example
☐	*equitable, resources, funds*	**allocation**	*n.*	The efficient *allocation* of capital . . .
☐		**assure**	*v.*	He *assured* us that human rights would be respected.
☐		**behalf**	*n.*	Institutions that are accountable to the people are supposed to function on *behalf* of those people.
☐		**collapse**	*n.*	Globalization may lead to the eventual *collapse* of the nation-state.
☐		**convention**	*n.*	It has been at the origin of several *conventions* and treaties.
☐		**currency**	*n.*	*Currency* crises are often triggered by a lot of speculators and global forces.
☐		**devote**	*v.*	They should *devote* more energy to strengthening local communities.
☐		**restrain**	*v.*	Individual states are critically weakened and cannot *restrain* corporate actions.

EXERCISE **2** Before reading the following passage, answer these questions.

1. How would you define globalization?

_____

_____

2. What does globalization include? Is it just about economics, or does it have a cultural or political component as well?

_____

_____

Reading 1

VOICES ON GLOBALIZATION

A. "Globalization is the process of increased political and economic control being taken by corporations, leading to the eventual **collapse** of the nation-state, thereby reducing nationality to irrelevance."

B. "Globalization is the process of increasing connectivity and interdependence in the world's markets and businesses."

C. "Since there is no mechanism for nations to act collectively, individual states are critically weakened and cannot **restrain** corporate actions. Globalization has facilitated the creation of a single market, without a single state to regulate it."

D. "There is a need for international, market-controlling institutions but they need to be democratic, representative and accountable to the people on whose **behalf** they are supposed to function. This will not be the case if international business is successful in its bid to hijack these institutions."

E. "A necessary complement to globalization is the Universal Declaration of Human Rights, which is today the best-kept secret in the world; it has been at the origin of several **conventions** and treaties which today form the corpus of international human rights law."

F. "Corporations in global capital markets perform an essential service by facilitating the efficient **allocation** of capital around the world."

G.   "We can change this world for the better. But to do that, we need certain principles, we need objectives, **assuring** all that international human rights are protected—we need commitment and we need action. Action at the individual level, and action collectively."

H.   "The really constructive response to globalization by those who feel that they benefit from it is to **devote** more energy to strengthening local communities, cohesion in the local community, prosperity in the local community, education and training in the local community."

I.   "**Currency** crises are often triggered by a lot of speculators and global forces—banks **collapse** in one country, which can quickly spread to its neighbors as well."

J.   "In these global transactions, money seems to come out of the air, the ether, and equally quickly banks suddenly **collapse**, and people have made millions in paper money on the stock exchange without a corresponding increase in anything that is measurable."

Sources of quotes:
A. http://pacific.commerce.ubc.ca/keith/Lectures/mne2.html
B. http://www.investorwords.com/2182/globalization.html
C. Cohen, M. G., Ritchie, L., Swenarchuk, M., & Vosko, L. *Globalization: Some Implications and Strategies for Women*, http://www3.sympatico.ca/truegrowth/womenstrat1.html
D. International Financier George Soros
E. and G. Amnesty International Secretary General Pierre Sane
F. and H. Vice Chairman, Goldman Sachs, International Andrew Hormats
I. Allan Nairn, Journalist, Indonesian Specialist;
J. Deputy President of South Africa Thabo Mbeki
All interviews from
http://www.globalvision.org/program/globalization/index.htm.

EXERCISE   3   Answer the following questions about Reading 1. In your answers, try to use the vocabulary words given in the parentheses.

1. In quote D, the speaker says that some institutions should be working on **behalf** of someone. What might those institutions be? Who are the people on whose **behalf** they should be working? (*behalf*)

_____

_____

_____

2. Do you think that globalization can lead to the **collapse** of nations, as suggested in quote A? Why or why not? (*collapse*)

_____

_____

_____

Master Student Tip

Flash cards and vocabulary notebooks are wonderful vocabulary tools. They can include any information you think is important to remember about a word. This information should include at least some of the eight ways to learn vocabulary: meanings, spoken form (pronunciation), written form (spelling), grammar, collocations, frequency, register, and associations.

- What type of information is included in the flash card about **allocation** in Exercise 4?
- What kinds of information do you find useful for your own vocabulary building?
- Do you prefer to use flash cards, a notebook, or some other learning tool?

EXERCISE 4 Make a flashcard for each bold vocabulary word in Word List 5.1. Use a dictionary to find or confirm definitions. Include information about the word's collocations and pronunciation.

Allocation (noun)   4-3 Stress pattern
DEF: The process of keeping some resources/money/time to use for
a specific purpose (FINANCE!)
COLLOCATIONS: Allocation of resources/land/time
              Modest/generous/limited allocation
              Increase/up or reduce/cut allocations of . . .
Formal: allocation   informal: setting something aside for . . .
WORD FAMILY: VERB: allocate   no adjective or adverb

EXERCISE 5 Answer these questions about the vocabulary words in the word bank. The first one has been done for you as an example.

allocation	behalf	convention	devote
assure	collapse	currency	restrain

1. _____ Which verb is often used with *time* or *money* as its object?

2. _____ Which word has a 4–3 pronunciation pattern?

3. _____ Which word is often in a three-word phrase, in which it follows *on* and comes before *of*?

4. _____ Which word is the opposite of *build* or *put up*?

5. _____ Which noun is most likely to be used in writing about international financial markets?

6. _____ Which verb means to guarantee?

7. _____ Which word can be a noun or a verb?

8. _____ Which word can be made into a noun by adding the final letter *t*?

9. _____ Which verb can be made into a noun with a suffix pronounced /shən/, like the sound at the end of *allocation* and *convention*?

10. _____ Which word are you most likely to use in your own writing? (Be prepared to explain why.)

Section 2

EXERCISE 6 For each bold vocabulary word in Word List 5.2, circle the letter of the best definition. Look at the examples, and use a dictionary if necessary.

WORD LIST 5.2

Word/Examples	Definitions
construct (*v.*) . . . *construct* a plan . . .	a. To destroy b. To encourage c. To build
invoke (*v.*) . . . they plan to *invoke* the case of . . . . . . *invoking* landmark rulings . . .	a. To worry about b. To require c. To refer to
so-called (*adj.*) . . . their *so-called* war of liberation . . . . . . *so-called* political movement . . .	a. Not really accurate b. Well-described c. Expensive
simulate (*v.*) . . . the flight machine *simulates* space travel . . . . . . how can we *simulate* the nuclear process rather than risk exposure . . .	a. To imitate b. To stop c. To forget
subsidiary (*n.*) . . . a wholly-owned *subsidiary* . . . The House of Commons would be a small *subsidiary* of the European Parliament.	a. The entire thing b. A smaller part of something big c. A corporation
trigger (*v.*) The drug *triggers* suicidal impulses. . . . the controversy which *triggered* the latest commotion . . .	a. To start something b. To continue to do something c. To finish something

Word/Examples	Definitions
undergo (*v.*) …after *undergoing* medical treatment … …language has *undergone* substantial changes …	a. To experience something b. To make something happen c. To avoid doing something
undertake (*adj.*) I've *undertaken* an enormous task. Venezuela is *undertaking* an expansion of its refineries.	a. To fall apart b. To decide to do something c. To return

EXERCISE **7** Before reading the following passage, answer these questions.

1. Do you consider globalization to be predominantly positive or negative?

_____

_____

2. What does it mean to have a safety net? What might the title "Globalization Without a Net" mean?

_____

_____

Reading 2

GLOBALIZATION WITHOUT A NET?

Debate over globalization often focuses on its impact on those people most vulnerable to sudden changes caused by new technologies, foreign competition, or industrial relocation. A new consensus is emerging around a simple, compelling proposition: Countries can harness the many benefits of global integration as long as they provide strong social protection programs that protect society's weakest members. This call for strengthened social protection **invokes** the post-WWII European governmental policies in which many nations erected formal, state-financed social protection systems to safeguard citizens from the risks linked to old age, illness, unemployment, and poverty.

Governments during that period began three innovative policy instruments to **construct** the modern welfare state: first, they spent public monies directly on social programs such as healthcare and unemployment compensation; second, they provided tax deductions on such expenses as interest payments on home mortgages and medical and educational costs, as a way to stimulate "socially desirable" spending by individuals; and third, they introduced regulations that would protect workers or other special groups, including minimum wage laws, rent controls, subsidized student loans, and reduced rates on public utilities.

Today, however, the growing integration of economies and the free movement of capital across borders threaten to undermine the effectiveness of these policy instruments. Even as the forces of globalization increase demand for strong social safety nets to protect the poor, these same forces also erode the ability of governments to **undertake** large-scale social welfare policies.

Consider the tax revenue needed to finance social spending. Although many industrialized economies have their fiscal houses in order, with tax revenues near historical highs, several "fiscal termites" linked to globalization are nevertheless gnawing at their foundations. These termites include increased travel by individuals, which allows them to purchase expensive and easily transportable items in countries or regions with low sales taxes, thereby encouraging small nations to reduce taxes on luxury products to attract foreign buyers. In addition, the growth of global e-commerce represents a nightmare for tax authorities since paperless, electronic transactions leave few footprints.

The growing use of offshore tax havens as conduits for financial investments likewise weakens national tax collection since individuals or corporations holding such assets—recently estimated at $5 trillion worldwide—are unlikely to report income from these assets to the tax authorities in their home countries. Another concern is that the growth of international trade among **subsidiaries** of the same multinational corporations further complicates tax collection, since companies can easily manipulate internal prices to keep profits in low-tax jurisdictions—**so-called** transfer pricing. For example, some analysts have questioned the high profits that multinational firms record as originating in Ireland (a country that happens to offer particularly low tax rates for corporations). Finally, downward pressure on tax rates will further restrict governments' ability to use tax policy for social protection. Corporate tax rates in industrialized nations show a decline from about 46 percent in 1985 to 33 percent in 1999, with tax rates for individuals **undergoing** a similar reduction. Computer **simulations** suggest that these trends will continue for at least the medium term. Put together, these elements will keep governments from maintaining current tax revenues, and may in fact **trigger** widespread spending cuts in social protection programs globally.

Of course, the competitive pressures of globalization, as well as the need to comply with new international agreements, may push policymakers to increase spending on education, training, research and development, the environment, and on reforming government institutions. Such initiatives likely would offer broad benefits to society as a whole. Ultimately, however, the process of global economic integration might require a fundamental overhaul of the role the state plays in pursuing social protection policies targeted toward specific groups—most critically, toward those adversely affected by the downsides of globalization.

Source: Tanzi, V. (2003). "Globalization Without a Net." *Global Politics in a Changing World: A Reader. (*Eds.) R. Mansbach and E. Rhodes. Boston: Houghton Mifflin, pp. 474–476.

EXERCISE 8 Answer the following questions about Reading 1. In your answers, try to use the vocabulary words given in the parentheses.

1. Why does the author use the phrase "so-called transfer pricing"? What do you think the author feels about this practice? What other practices or activities would you use *so-called* about? (*so-called*)

_____

_____

_____

_____

2. Why would people discussing globalization **invoke** policies that were adopted at the end of World War II? What connections are there between that period and the current discussion about globalization? (*invoke*)

_____

_____

_____

_____

EXERCISE **9** Rewrite the following spoken sentences. Find the idea or words that you can replace with the word in parentheses, and underline them. Then write the sentence in appropriate written academic English. The first one has been done for you as an example.

"After the Second World War, governments across Europe started three exciting new social programs. You see, what they were really doing was <u>putting together</u> what we now call the modern welfare state." Political science class (<u>construct</u>)	European governments during the period after World War II initiated three innovative social programs to <u>construct</u> the modern welfare state.
"They ran temperature analysis, and it shows the same negative results that have come from using computers to look at where we are going with greenhouse gas emissions." Political science class (<u>simulation</u>)	
"So we would need to know a lot more about what kind of research has been going on in the United Kingdom." Sociology class (<u>undertaken</u>)	
"They were asking for the right to conduct, if you can forgive the contradiction, peaceful nuclear explosions, which many did not think was viable or acceptable." History class (<u>so-called</u>)	

"Janet was a secretary, and she spent some time in front of a computer screen, and her office was lit with strip-lights. Both of these have been shown to quickly start migrainous attacks." Pre-med class (*triggered*)	
"A lot of the data that you've pulled off the World Wide Web has not really been through the kind of scripting that you'd expect from a peer review scholarly publishers." Computer science class (*undergone*)	

Source: Some quotes from Pat Byrd's corpus of spoken academic English.

Master Student Tip

When you learn a word, try to determine its register (whether it is primarily spoken or written, and its level of formality). In Exercise 10, you should have noticed that many academic words have meanings similar to those of other less formal words. Using academic language tells your reader that you understand the differences between speaking and writing, and between a casual letter and an academic paper.

What pairs of words in Exercise 10 have similar meanings but are in different registers?

Formal	Informal

Section 3

EXERCISE 10 For each bold vocabulary word in Word List 5.3, write a short definition. Look at the examples, and use a dictionary to check your work.

WORD LIST 5.3

Word/Examples	Definition
accommodate (*v.*) The Web *accommodates* significant national and linguistic differences.	
coherence (*n.*) ... the ideas are taken together and put into a *coherent* plan ... ... maintain a certain intellectual *coherence* ...	
found (*v.*) Bill Gates left college to *found* Microsoft with Paul Allen. The university, *founded* in 1640, is among the oldest in the United States.	
hierarchy (*n.*) We should order the ideas in a *hierarchy* that enables people to see the relationship. ... he quickly moved up the *hierarchy* ...	
innovation (*n.*) There's no logical reason why the United States should have a monopoly on Internet *innovation*.	
odd (*adj.*) How *odd*! ... the *odd* thing is that ...	

Word/Examples	Definition
predominantly (*adv.*) . . . a *predominantly* middle-class neighborhood . . . . . . black students at a *predominantly* white university . . .	
subordinate (*v.*) . . . a culture that *subordinates* social responsibility to getting very, very rich . . . The needs of individuals are largely *subordinated* to the needs of the community.	

EXERCISE 11 Before reading the following passage, answer these questions.

1. What do you use the Internet for? What languages do you use when you are using the Internet?

_____

_____

_____

2. Do you think the Internet has a nationality? Why or why not?

_____

_____

_____

3. "The Internet is profoundly disrespectful of tradition, estblished order and hierarchy, and that is very American." Do you agree with this statement? Why or why not?

_____

_____

_____

Reading 3

WELCOME TO THE INTERNET, THE FIRST GLOBAL COLONY

In the beginning, there was Pangaea, the Earth's great land mass, which broke up 240 million years ago as Earth's tectonic plates moved apart. That was the last global continent, until now. The Internet is the new cyber-Pangaea. While this new global realm is **predominantly** U.S. territory, the **odd** thing is that many pioneering breakthroughs came from abroad. The World Wide Web, for example, was created by an Oxford-educated physicist, Tim Berners-Lee, at a physics laboratory in Switzerland. Mr. Berners-Lee, however, like so many emigrant technologists, soon departed for the more fertile soil of America, where the **innovations** of the Internet have flourished. The causes cited by way of explanation are all ingredients that contribute to the entrepreneurial climate in the United States—venture capital financing, close ties between business and universities, flexible labor markets, a deregulated business environment, and a culture that **subordinates** social responsibility to getting very, very rich.

The result is that the technology, economics, and culture of the Internet feel awfully American. English is the dominant language of the Internet, found on most Web sites and used in most e-mail. Perhaps most important, the culture of the Net tends to be informal and individualistic, decentralized with little apparent **coherence** or central control. This makes it the preferred medium of dissident groups in countries around the world, and it also makes it feel just like home to American Net surfers. "The Internet is profoundly disrespectful of tradition, established order and **hierarchy**, and that is very American," observed Fareed Zakaria, the managing editor of *Foreign Affairs*.

Many nations are concerned, however, that the Internet economy may prove impossible to regulate, and may create such vast inequality and rootlessness among its citizens that they will lose their sense of social cohesion. Like much of America's influence on the world, the Internet lies in the arena of what Joseph S. Nye, dean of Harvard University's Kennedy School of Government terms "soft power." It's like rock 'n' roll or American movies, which earn lots of money, to be sure, but mainly influence other nations by offering an irresistible alternative culture.

Still, despite America's early Internet lead, the Web is a vast expanse, **accommodating** significant national and linguistic differences. Today, nearly half of the global online population resides in the United States, but this edge in Internet use is expected to decline steadily as other countries, especially Europe and Japan, close the gap. Some industry executives believe Europe could quickly catch or perhaps even surpass America in Internet technology as the world moves beyond the personal computer into the coming "post-PC era," during which, Nye says, people will increasingly use wireless devices like "smart" cell phones for e-mail, shopping and information services over the Internet.

But it is culture—not raw technology alone—that will determine whether the United States retains its status as the pre-eminent Internet nation. David Braunschvig, a managing director of Lazard Freres & Company, is optimistic about Europe and he insists "there is no logical reason why the U.S. should have this de facto monopoly on Internet **innovation**."

Mr. Braunschvig, whose doctorate in computer science is from the University of Paris, says he tells his friends at dinner parties in France that all Europe with its 350 million people really needs to produce is 30 or 40 entrepreneurs like Marc Andreessen, who left college to **co-found** Netscape, the Internet browser pioneer. "My European friends say, Of course, we've produced such people, but they have moved to America," says Mr. Braunschvig, who lives in New York.

Source: Lohr, S. (2003). "Welcome to the Internet, the First Global Colony." *Global Politics in a Changing World: A Reader.* (Eds.) R. Mansbach and E. Rhodes. Boston: Houghton Mifflin, pp. 486–488.

EXERCISE 12 Answer the following questions about Reading 3. In your answers, try to use the vocabulary words given in the parentheses.

1. What factors determine where new ideas on the Internet come from? (*innovation*)

_____

_____

_____

2. The author uses the example of Netscape co-founder Marc Andreessen as one innovative European in the Internet. Do an Internet search to find out more about the founders of several "new technology" companies. Be prepared to discuss your results. (*innovative, found*)

_____

_____

_____

Master Student Tip

Using a vocabulary notebook can be a very useful tool. Every learner has her or his own learning style, so the best notebook for you may be quite different from a notebook that works well for another student. Regardless of your learning style, however, consider the following in creating and organizing a vocabulary notebook:

- Is it easy to modify? Can you take pages in and out or move them around?
- How do you plan to organize the words—alphabetically? by subject? by difficulty?
- What areas do you think you need to work on? Some students may need to spend more energy on spelling or word formation; others may not need to work on those.
- How do you address the eight ways of building vocabulary? Do you distinguish between your receptive and productive vocabulary knowledge?
- Do you include authentic samples of the words taken from readings that you are interested in or that are important to your studies?

Can you think of other questions you should consider when creating and updating a vocabulary notebook?

EXERCISE **13** Answer these questions about the vocabulary words in the word bank. The first one has been done for you as an example.

accommodate	found	innovation	predominantly
coherence	hierarchy	odd	subordinate

1. ___*hierarchy*___ Which noun can be used to describe the structure of an organization?

2. _____ Which word is related to being clear and well thought out?

3. _____ Which word is an adverb?

4. _____ Which word has a 3–2 pronunciation pattern?

5. _____ Which verb is spelled the same way as the past tense of a common verb meaning "to locate something"?

6. _____ Which word can be a noun, an adjective, or a verb?

7. _____ Which word has the most meanings?

8. _____ Which word has the most syllables?

9. _____ Which word begins with a prefix that means "under"?

10. _____ For you, which word is the most difficult to spell? What can you do to make it easier?

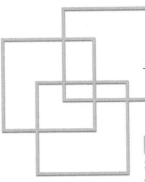

Section 4

CHAPTER 5 REVIEW

EXERCISE 14 Review the Chapter 5 Word List. Do you know the meaning of each word? Do you know the part of speech? What different word forms do the words have? What options do you have if you want to use informal speech for the same idea?

advocate	erode	intervene	overlap
allocation	behalf	convention	devote
assure	collapse	currency	restrain
construct	invoke	so-called	simulate
subsidiary	trigger	undergo	undertake
accommodate	coherence	found	hierarchy
innovation	odd	predominantly	subordinate

EXERCISE 15 Write the best word from the row to complete each sentence. Use a dictionary to check your work.

coherent	subordinate	restrained	predominant	innovative

1. In any case, environmental issues usually played only a/an
   _____ role in policy-making. Concern for impact on the
   land, air, and water was rarely a serious consideration until very late
   in the twentieth century, if then.

2. The aim of the guidelines is to set out a clear role for each committee
   within a _____, sensible framework.

3. After her flamboyant excesses of the 1920s, she started designing
   new shapes in the 1930s, and her colors and designs grew more
   _____.

4. I believe that the project is so exciting, _____, and
   imaginative that it should be approached on a bipartisan level.

allocation	subsidiary	currency	assurance	hierarchy

5. This was in addition to problems in Brazil, where the "plainly volatile" economic and _____ situation led to a 16 percent fall in volume at BAT's Souza Cruz <u>subsidiary</u>.

6. And then there was this caveat that said the further you get up the _____, the closer you get to genuine policy-making.

7. They have also demanded the elimination from the county budget of a $400,000 _____ to study wolves over a five-year period.

8. Significantly, he gave no _____ that the factory would remain open and that the workers would keep their jobs.

EXERCISE 16 Complete the chart by writing word forms for each bold vocabulary word's part of speech. If no word form exists, write "none." After you are done, compare your answers with another student's. Then check in a dictionary for other forms of these words. The first one has been done for you as an example.

Noun	Verb	Adjective	Adverb
accommodation	**accommodate**	accommodating	none
	construct		
innovation			
	simulate		
convention			
	devote		
allocation			

WEB POWER

You will find additional exercises related to the content in this chapter at **http://esl.college.hmco.com/students.**

6

The Environment

In this chapter, you will

- Become familiar with twenty-four high-frequency academic English words
- Examine the range of meanings of these words
- Look at collocation patterns
- Read about environmental issues

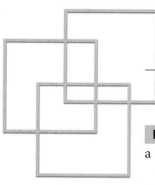

Section 1

EXERCISE **1** For each bold vocabulary word in Word List 6.1, write a short definition. Look at the examples, and use a dictionary if necessary.

Word/Examples	Definition
contradiction (*n.*) …in direct *contradiction* to what you said earlier … …a basic *contradiction* … …a *contradiction* in terms …	
displacement (*n.*) …the largest *displacement* of people in the past two years … …determined by *displacement* by a liquid …	
extract (*v.*) It uses cyanide to help *extract* gold from ore … …a number of systems were developed to *extract* information about terrorists …	
infrastructure (*n.*) …industries needed to make use of the existing *infrastructure* … …building of much needed *infrastructure* such as roads, garbage disposal, and water …	
inherent (*adj.*) …it reveals *inherent* contradictions between one side and the other … …inevitable difficulties *inherent* in a study of this nature …	

Word/Examples	Definition
notwithstanding (*prep.*) The employer expressly assures employees that, *notwithstanding* the existence of an employee program, they are free to select traditional union representation. This was the case *notwithstanding* the fact that all the information given to the expert had been previously published.	
overlap (*v.*) It is just that so many desirable ends are incompatible, or, if interests *overlap*, they do not necessarily coincide. The different dimensions of conflict *overlap* and interact in a sometimes bewildering variety of ways.	
preceding (*adj.*) ...the audited accounts for the *preceding* financial year... ...the index was up 3.5 percent from the *preceding* month...	

EXERCISE 2   Before reading the following passage, answer these questions.

1. Look at the title of Reading 1, about environmental issues: What is the market economy? Why do you think the title includes the word *collision*?

_____

_____

2. Look at the illustrations of "ecological footprints." What does it mean to leave a footprint?

_____

_____

Reading 1

WORLDS IN COLLISION: THE MARKET ECONOMY IN THE 21ST CENTURY

The Market Economy. In considering the eventual development of a sustainable world economy, it is useful to examine three co-existing and **overlapping** economies: the market economy, the survival economy, and Nature's economy. As these economies move into even greater collision, politicians and corporate executives will be called upon to institute more effective policies and business strategies.

Let us first turn to the market economy, the familiar world of commerce, compromising both developed nations and "emerging economy" nations. Most energy use (and misuse) occurs in affluent societies of the developed nations, whose 1 billion people use more than 75% of the world's energy. **Notwithstanding** this intense use of energy and massive **extraction** of natural resources, levels of pollution remain relatively low in developed nations. This apparent **contradiction** has three main causes: strict environmental law, growing corporate awareness of green issues, and a shift in pollution-generating activities to emerging economy nations.

An **inherent** result of this shift of pollution-generating activities, such as heavy manufacturing and the processing of natural resources, from developed nations to emerging economy nations has been an enormous **displacement** of rural peoples, as they move towards jobs in new megacities throughout these nations. Such urbanization presents unprecedented challenges to economic infrastructures and the environment. Enormous success in the market economy may be leading to a possible collapse in the 'hidden' economies: the survival economy and the economy of the planet itself.

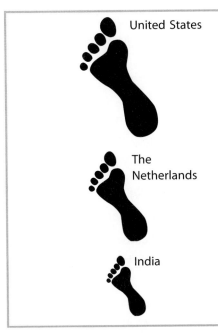

United States

The Netherlands

India

"In the United States, it takes 12.2 acres to supply the average person's basic needs; in the Netherlands, 8 acres; in India, 1 acre. The Dutch ecological footprint covers 15 times the area of the Netherlands, whereas India's footprint exceeds its area by only about 35%. Most strikingly, if the entire world lived like North Americans, it would take three planet Earths to support the present world population." Stuart L. Hart.

Source: Hart, S. L. (1999). "Beyond Greening: Strategies for a Sustainable World." *Environmental Management Readings and Cases.* (Ed.) M. V. Russo. Boston: Houghton Mifflin, pp. 2–14.

EXERCISE   3   Answer the following questions based on Reading 1. In your answers, try to use the vocabulary words given in the parentheses.

1. What are some of the unprecedented challenges to infrastructure caused by the movement of people from rural to urban areas? (*unprecedented, infrastructure*)

_____

_____

_____

2. What can be done to address the apparent contradiction that those nations with the highest resource exploitation feel few of its ill effects? (*contradiction*)

_____

_____

_____

EXERCISE 4 Change the following words into another form. The first one has been done for you as an example. Use a dictionary to check your work.

		→
contradiction	noun to verb	_to contradict_
contradiction	noun to adjective	_____
preceding	adjective to verb	_____
extract	verb to noun	_____
displacement	noun to verb	_____
inherent	adjective to adverb	_____
overlap	verb to adjective	_____

→

EXERCISE 5 Write stress patterns for the following words. The first one has been done for you as an example. After you are done, use a dictionary to check your work.

1. contradiction (__4__ – __3__)

2. extract (_v._) (_____ – _____)

3. contradicts (_____ – _____)

4. extracted (_____ – _____)

5. inherently (_____ – _____)

6. preceding (_____ – _____)

7. displacement (_____ – _____)

8. contradictory (_____ – _____)

9. precedent (_____ – _____)

10. extract (_n._) (_____ – _____)

11. inherent (_____ – _____)

12. preceded (_____ – _____)

13. displace (_____ – _____)

14. precedence (_____ – _____)

15. unprecedented (_____ – _____)

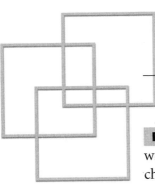

Section 2

EXERCISE 6 For each bold vocabulary word in Word List 6.2, write a short definition. Read the examples, and use a dictionary to check your work.

WORD LIST 6.2

Word/Examples	Definition
erosion (*n.*) The land, as the result of soil *erosion*, can no longer support the population. . . . the *erosion* of family values . . .	
incompatible (*adj.*) They are completely *incompatible* with NATO's defense policies. . . . wild social hours are simply *incompatible* with family life . . .	
intensity (*n.*) . . . the world glowed with an *intensity* that made his body ache . . . . . . sunspots will increase in frequency and *intensity* in September . . .	
manual (*adj.*) . . . *manual* transmission . . . . . . *manual* labor is often difficult, dangerous, and poorly paid . . .	
orientation (*n.*) . . . sexual *orientation* . . . . . . political *orientation* . . .	
pose (*v.*) . . . that *poses* a threat . . . . . . that really *poses* a problem . . .	

Word/Examples	Definition
prohibit (*v.*) ...expressly *prohibit* ... ...federal law *prohibits* smoking in public places ... ...you are *prohibited* from gambling ...	
widespread (*adj.*) ...there has been *widespread* concern ... ...the incident triggered *widespread* charges of police corruption ...	

EXERCISE 7 Before reading the following passage, answer this question.

You have already read about the market economy. What other economies might exist?

_____

_____

_____

Reading 2

WORLDS IN COLLISION: POVERTY AND THE ENVIRONMENT

The *Survival Economy and Nature's Economy.* The second overlapping economy is the survival economy, which contains about 3 billion people, mainly Africans, Indians, and Chinese who are subsistence-**oriented** (surviving from day to day) and utilize **intensive manual** labor to meet their basic needs directly from nature. **Widespread** poverty and hunger **prohibit** those in this economy from seriously considering environmental issues. Short-term needs are often **incompatible** with long-term environmental issues, resulting in deforestations, soil erosion, and water contamination.

In contrast with the market economy and the survival economy, which are both people-driven, Nature's economy consists of the natural systems and resources that allow both the market and survival economies to exist. Two main resources comprise this economy: renewable and non-renewable natural resources. Surprisingly, the greatest risk to our planet may be **posed** by the depletion of renewable rather than non-renewable resources. Through technology, many common non-renewable resources are being replaced by renewable alternatives.

The interdependence between these three economies is growing stronger over time and will require innovative leadership from government and business. The challenge for humankind in the foreseeable future is how to integrate these economies in a sustainable and humane way, thereby circumventing catastrophes in climate change, pollution, poverty, and inequality.

Source: Hart, S. L. (1999). "Beyond Greening: Strategies for a Sustainable World." *Environmental Management Readings and Cases.* (Ed.) M. V. Russo. Boston: Houghton Mifflin, pp. 2–14.

EXERCISE 8 Answer the following questions based on Reading 2. In your answers, try to use the vocabulary words given in the parentheses.

1. In what ways do these two economies overlap with the market economy? (*overlap*)

_____

_____

_____

_____

2. What short-term needs might result in soil *erosion* in the survival economy? How might this erosion be prevented? (*erosion*)

_____

_____

_____

_____

Master Student Tip

Building collocation awareness is an important skill, especially in writing. Collocations are words that are frequently used together. Many words have collocations, and equally important, they have other words that are not collocations. For example, the words *tall* and *high* are similar, yet *tall* collocates with *man* and *building* (a tall man, a tall building but **not** high man, high building), but not with *profile*, *price*, or *altitude* (high profile, high price, high altitude but **not** tall profile, tall price, tall altitude).

Why are collocations important? They are used for natural-sounding communication; being able to use these effectively allows people to listen to your **message** rather than the groups of words you use.

Notice the following nouns often used after the adjective *widespread*:

widespread **abuses**	widespread **discrimination**	widespread **poverty**
widespread **criticism**	widespread **fraud**	widespread **violence**
widespread **looting**	widespread **discontent**	widespread **corruption**

An important part of building vocabulary is noticing patterns of words. What do you notice about all these words modified by *widespread*?

EXERCISE 9 Answer the following questions about *widespread*.

1. What kinds of nouns does *widespread* modify? Predict the best way to use *widespread* in your own writing.

_____

_____

2. Use your prediction to help you decide which words listed below probably do not collocate with *widespread*. Cross out those words. The first one has been done for you as an example.

~~serenity~~	apprehension	concern	celebration
speculation	confusion	fears	infrastructure
opposition	peace	guidelines	certainty

3. If you were going to write a sentence starting with the following phrase, would you complete it with a positive statement or a negative statement?

There was a widespread belief that . . .

_____

Now, read these authentic texts:

i. . . . Such taxes, however, did not bring money into the papal coffers but were given to the leaders of the crusades, though there was a *widespread* belief that money collected for the Crusade by Philip the notary was doing exactly that, and in 1202 Innocent ordered an investigation.

ii. His office arrested an alleged second gunman in the case last week, confirming *widespread* belief that Colosio had been killed by conspirators.

iii. I have to warn the Chancellor that there is a *widespread* belief that he is not at all likely to take the measures that might prove necessary if intervention is insufficient to stem severe downward pressure on sterling in the coming months.

EXERCISE 10 With a partner, match each bold vocabulary word with its group of collocates (words that frequently occur together). Write the vocabulary word in the blank. Make your best guess by looking at the entire group of collocates. After you have completed the exercise, check your answers by asking proficient speakers of English or by using a dictionary.

1. widespread	**a.** ADJ + NOUN: high/low _____
2. manual	VERB *in* NOUN: increase/decrease in _____
3. intensity	**b.** ADV + ADJ: extremely/increasingly _____
4. prohibited	ADJ + NOUN: _____ concern/violence/damage/speculation/ fear/support
5. orientation	**c.** ADJ + NOUN: sexual/ideological/political/religious _____
6. incompatible	**d.** ADJ + NOUN: _____ transmission/labor/workers
	ADV + ADJ + NOUN: skilled/unskilled _____ labor/workers
	e. ADV + ADJ: expressly/strictly/constitutionally _____
	VERB (passive) *from* GERUND: someone is _____ from VERB *-ing*

Master Student Tip

A useful tool for building collocation awareness is a collocation dictionary. This type of dictionary does not have definitions, but instead lists the words that most frequently collocate with many common words, including almost all the words on the Academic Word List. You can find a useful list of such dictionaries by searching for *ESL collocation dictionaries* in an online search engine.

Section 3

EXERCISE 11 For each bold vocabulary word in Word List 6.3, write a short definition. Read the examples, and use a dictionary to check your work.

WORD LIST 6.3

Word/Examples	Definition
advocate (*v.*) We talked about ways we could *advocate* for education. . . . we still *advocate* sticking with growth stocks . . .	
coincide (*v.*) . . . this was timed to *coincide* with Memorial Day celebrations . . . . . . unfortunately, your needs and mine don't always *coincide* . . .	
conformity (*n.*) . . . we took swift and decisive action in *conformity* with the President's wishes . . . . . . the 1950s were a decade of sockhops and *conformity* . . .	
induce (*v.*) . . . a drug-*induced* stupor . . . . . . the music seemed to *induce* a state of relaxation . . . . . . it can *induce* a powerful allergic response in children . . .	

Word/Examples	Definition
intervention (*n.*) The new government stated it would not accept any foreign *intervention*. . . . they met to discuss an appropriate *intervention* to reduce infant mortality . . .	
intrinsic (*adj.*) There was *intrinsic* pleasure in watching the old films. . . . fighting was an *intrinsic* part of the male code . . . . . . the prints themselves have no *intrinsic* value . . .	
justification (*n.*) I see no *justification* for the price increase. . . . the *justification* given was . . .	
unify (*v.*) Europe has been *unified* by a single currency. . . . this common issue could *unify* Democrats and Republicans . . .	

EXERCISE **12** Before reading the following passage, answer these questions.

1. What factors do you consider when shopping for food and other purchases? Are you willing to pay more for environmentally sound products?

   _____

   _____

2. For what reasons might some people be willing to pay extra for such products?

   _____

   _____

Reading 3

THE MANY SHADES OF "GREEN" CONSUMERS

Green consumers do not present a **unified** front in their beliefs or spending habits. There are five main categories used when measuring consumers' degree of environmental concern, three considered green and two considered 'brown.' There is, nonetheless, some overlap between the various categories, especially as more information is made available.

Shades of Green – US Consumers

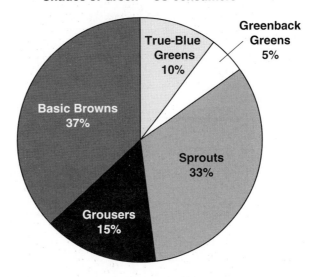

The greenest consumers are "True-Blues," who have intense beliefs about the **intrinsic** value of preserving the environment. This group will often pay a considerable premium for environmentally sound products. They are politically and socially active, and have been the strongest **advocates** for changes not only in buying patterns but also in lifestyle changes. These consumers believe that greater government **intervention** is necessary to improve management of resources by industry.

The second group is the "Greenbacks," so named for their willingness to spend money on environmentally preferable products, but who also display a reluctance to change their lifestyle. The third group is the "Sprouts," who can be **induced** to buy green when it **coincides** with their own interests and only if it requires little sustained effort. The most common activity for this group is curbside recycling, when provided at no charge by local government.

Of the remaining consumers, the next group is the "Grousers." This group is adamant about not getting involved with green activities; they **justify** this stance by questioning the validity, quality, and cost of such activities. Finally, the largest group is the "Basic Browns." These consumers **conform** most closely to the market economy, they do not participate in green activities, and they are largely indifferent to environmental issues. There is some movement between these categories, but over the past 10 years, the percentage of consumers in each category has remained essentially unchanged. For environmentalists in the 21st century, one critical challenge will be to convince consumers to change their color from brown to green.

Source: Ottman, J. (1999). "Consumers with a Conscience." *Environmental Management Readings and Cases.* (Ed.) M. V. Russo. Boston: Houghton Mifflin, pp. 187–192.

EXERCISE 13   Answer the following questions based on Reading 3. In your answers, try to use the vocabulary words given in the parentheses.

1. Which of the five categories are you in? Why? Justify your position as a consumer. (*justify*)

   _____

   _____

   _____

   _____

2. Imagine you are an executive for a company that produces food products. Use the information in Reading 3 to justify advocating either for or against the marketing of "green" products. (*advocate*)

   _____

   _____

   _____

   _____

EXERCISE 14 Complete the chart by writing word forms for each bold vocabulary word's part of speech. If no word form exists, write "none." After you are done, compare your answers with another student's. Then check in a dictionary for other forms of these words. The first one has been done for you as an example.

Noun	Verb	Adjective	Adverb
advocacy	**advocate**	*none*	*none*
	coincide		
conformity			
	induce		
intervention			
		intrinsic	
justification			
	unify		

Master Student Tip

Another good source for collocation information is a dictionary. A good ESL/EFL learner dictionary, such as *The American Heritage English as a Second Language Dictionary*, provides collocation information for many words. Different dictionaries present this information in different places:

- The first and easiest place is a separate list of collocations placed near the entry for the word.
- Another place is in a secondary entry below the main entry. Sometimes multi-word entries occur after the main entry, which include idiomatic phrases and very strong collocations.
- A final place to find useful collocations is in the example sections of the entry. Good dictionaries include the most common structures and collocates in the examples for words.

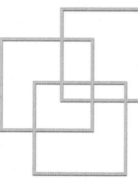

Section 4

CHAPTER 6 REVIEW

EXERCISE 15 Review the Chapter 6 Word List. Do you know the meaning(s) of each word? Do you know the part of speech? What different word forms do the words have? How do you pronounce them? What collocations do they have?

advocate	erosion	intervention	overlap
coincide	extract	intrinsic	pose
incompatible	induce	justification	preceding
conformity	infrastructure	manual	prohibit
contradiction	inherent	notwithstanding	unify
displacement	intensity	orientation	widespread

EXERCISE 16 Write stress patterns for the following words. The first one is done for you as an example. Use a dictionary to check your work.

1. advocate   (__3__ – __/__)

2. coincide   (_____ – _____)

3. conformity   (_____ – _____)

4. induce   (_____ – _____)

5. intervention   (_____ – _____)

6. intrinsic   (_____ – _____)

7. justification   (_____ – _____)

8. unify   (_____ – _____)

9. advocacy   (_____ – _____)

10. coincidentally   (_____ – _____)

11. nonconformist   (_____ – _____)

12. inductive   (_____ – _____)

13. intervene   (_____ – _____)

EXERCISE 17 It is important that you can use different word forms to rephrase ideas represented by academic words. Review each excerpt from the readings in this chapter, and write a new sentence using the word form provided. The first one has been done for you as an example.

1. It is useful to examine three co-existing and <u>overlapping</u> economies: the market economy, the survival economy, and Nature's economy. **overlap (verb)**

   It is useful to examine the three economies (the market economy, the survival economy, and Nature's economy) that co-exist and overlap.

2. These consumers believe that great government <u>intervention</u> is necessary to improve management of resources by industry. **intervene (verb)**

   _____

   _____

3. The Grousers <u>justify</u> this stance by questioning the validity, quality, and cost of such activities. **justification (noun)**

   _____

   _____

4. An <u>inherent</u> result of this shift has been an <u>enormous displacement</u> of rural peoples. **displace (verb)**

   _____

   _____

5. The True Blues have been the strongest <u>advocates</u> for changes not only in buyng patterns but also in lifestyle changes. **advocate (verb)**

   _____

   _____

W E B   P O W E R

You will find additional exercises related to the content in this chapter at **http://esl.college.hmco.com/students.**

DATE DUE

SEP 0 8 2005	
APR 2 9 2009	